BATTLEFIELD WISDOM

TOP TIPS FOR BUSY PARENTS

NIGEL LATTA

D1388415

H46 540 574 5

First published 2012
HarperCollins*Publishers (New Zealand) Limited*
P.O. Box 1, Auckland 1140

Parts of this book were originally published in *How to Have Kids and Stay Sane* (2007)

HarperCollins*Publishers*
31 View Road, Glenfield, Auckland 0627, New Zealand
Level 13, 201 Elizabeth Street, Sydney, NSW 2000, Australia
A 53, Sector 57, Noida, UP, India
77–85 Fulham Palace Road, London W6 8JB, United Kingdom
2 Bloor Street East, 20th floor, Toronto, Ontario M4W 1A8, Canada
10 East 53rd Street, New York, NY 10022, USA

National Library of New Zealand Cataloguing-in-Publication Data

Latta, Nigel, 1967–
Battlefield wisdom : top tips for busy parents / Nigel Latta.
ISBN 978-1-86950-967-5
1. Parenting. 2. Parent and child. 3. Child rearing.
I. Title.649.1—dc 23

ISBN: 978 1 86950 967 5

Cover design and internal typesetting by IslandBridge
Cover photography by Charlie Smith

Printed by Printlink, Wellington, on 100gsm Offset

Contents

1
So you want to be a good parent, huh?

Yeah, well, good luck with that.

When my son was born I made a brief attempt at being a 'good parent'. I'm a professional, a clinical psychologist, and I'd been working with families for over a decade by then. I thought it was going to be easy. So off I set, convinced that I'd be a very 'good parent'. I'd spent years being paid to tell other people how to raise their kids. I was qualified and motivated; how hard could it be?

I tried hard to be a 'good parent', damn hard, and to my credit almost made two weeks.

The crunch came one afternoon when my wife was going out for a couple of hours to pretend she was still a real person and still had a life. Despite her misgivings, I was left in charge, pretty much by default because there was no one else. There were lists covering every eventuality from puking to tsunamis. It was supposed to be quality time for me and the boy. That was the plan anyway. To be fair we had at least a good 20 minutes of quality time. I made stupid faces, he made odd facial expressions (mostly, I suspect, from wind) and that was OK for a while. Then the novelty of 'quality time' wore off. There's only so much quality time you can have with someone who can't control their bowels.

The next step, obviously, was the television. We'd bought

one of those Mozart videos for babies, with the interesting visuals that are supposed to make your kid's brain grow. I knew it was complete nonsense, but if we hadn't and he'd turned out to be a bit of a thicky then I'd have never heard the end of it from his mother. We watched it for about 10 minutes. It was dull. Very dull. Then it moved beyond dull into the realms of utter tedium, and finally into the no-man's-land of just plain annoying.

And here's where we reached the crunch point, my boy and me, because I knew a 'good parent' would soldier on. A 'good parent' would sit and watch the whole thing while saying the colours out loud and being suitably encouraging. A 'good parent' would sing, and count, and jiggle and STIMULATE their precious little one's BRAIN DEVELOPMENT.

We sat there for a bit, me and my boy. I knew that my next step was important. Whatever I did next would set the tone for the whole parenting experience.

Finally, after thinking it all through, after reflecting on all that I'd learned about infant development and neonatal neurobiology, and all that I'd learned from over a decade of working with all kinds of families, I looked down at my infant son whose life and psychological wellbeing his mother had entrusted to me. This would be my defining moment as a parent. This was where I would discover what kind of parent I really was.

'Little man,' I said, quietly, my voice tender, filled with the soft warm tones of the wise old father, 'shall we watch Arnie in *Terminator 2* instead of this stupid baby crap?'

He was as keen as I was. Honestly.

So we ditched the alleged brain development nonsense and watched the Governor of California blow shit up instead. It was quality time in the truest sense of the word. My, how we bonded.

From that moment on I promised to forget all that 'good parent' nonsense and just be a plain old parent instead. My parents had just been plain old parents, and that seemed to go pretty well for me and my brothers and sister. None of us had died and no one lost an eye, although having said that I do have a scar on my knee from falling off a bike, and I also nearly cut off my little brother's finger in a gold-sluicing machine. Long story. It should be noted, however, that neither of these two misfortunes was my parents' fault.

If you try to be a 'good parent' you will go mad, die, or simply turn into a painfully boring person. The rest of us will find you very annoying. You will show off little Tarquin's extraordinary ability to poke out his tongue, and we will secretly wish you'd just shut up. We will look at you and, even though we will be smiling and nodding, secretly we will be thinking that you are a big fat pain in the arse.

We will feel sorry for your children.

'Good parents', in the modern sense of the phrase, are plain painful. So instead of telling you a hundred different ways to become one of the Stepford parents, and therefore a hundred different ways to feel guilty and inadequate, this book gives you the skinny on how to be a plain old parent.

Trust me, it's better this way.

2
That pounding sensation in your brain

Ever get that feeling? You know the one I mean: when you're so angry with your kids that you can actually feel the blood throbbing in the major arteries that supply your brain? This is an alarming sensation, because you know that it's probably the kind of feeling people get just before their brain bursts and squirts out their ears as they collapse lifeless to the ground.

This feeling is the first time you realize your children have the power to kill you out of sheer, unadulterated, unsustainable frustration. This is the first time it dawns on you that actually *you* might be the one who doesn't make it.

Having said that, on a bad day the idea of instant death from brain explosion might not seem like such a bad thing.

They wind us up, our little ones. We love them, but oh how they wind us up sometimes. It's worse if there are two. If there are two you're in real trouble brain-wise, because they hunt in packs. If there are two, they will stand one each side and let you have a double dose. It might be whining, it might be endless questions, it could just be inane little-kid banter. Whatever it is, you can be sure that two is definitely worse than one.

I remember about a month ago I became so angry, so enraged, at the ridiculousness of the latest dispute between my two boys that I actually had to go lie down. My head was pounding as the blood rushed about looking for somewhere to go. I could feel the arteries that supply vital parts of my brain creaking under the strain.

And what caused all this? From memory it was a completely insane dispute over an empty cardboard box that had been lying around largely ignored for the past month. On that particular day, though, it was the most valued, most prized possession in the entire world, and they both wanted it with the self-same passion that Gollum wanted the Ring. There was shrieking, and demanding, and pleading, and shoving, and the repeated blows thrown from one to the other. The utter ridiculousness of it, combined with the length of time the whole thing went on, almost killed me.

We all end up in that place sooner or later, and sadly most of us will make a large number of return trips over the years. We all get angry at our children, and sometimes the anger is so intense we become slightly dizzy, and we hear a high-pitched ringing in our ears. If you don't go there from time to time, you're probably not spending enough time with your children.

Having said all that, it's a dangerous place to be, because if you stay there too long it will literally take years off your life. So here are my top three tips for trying to go there less, and getting out quicker when you do.

Get a plan The big reason most parents feel enraged is because they feel powerless, because they're at the end of their proverbial tether, because nothing they've done has made any difference up until that point. Most of us don't want to be angry: we just end up feeling that way because it's the last refuge of a sane mind. The utter helplessness of being ignored by tiny little people is inherently enraging.

So you need to get a plan.

The plan doesn't have to be complicated. In fact, the best plans are the simplest ones. Just figure out where things start going pear-shaped, figure out what the little person is getting out of behaving that way, and then figure out how you can make them think again.

Distract them, remind them that if they do what you want they get a sticker on their chart, tell them if they keep doing what they're doing they'll end up in time out — or any one of a number of things. It doesn't matter what you do necessarily, so long as you do something. If you have a plan, you'll feel like you're in charge — and that will have magical calming qualities. If you don't have a plan, you'll just react — and generally when we just react, we react emotionally, and generally that emotion is anger.

Keep it all in context Sometimes it's very easy to believe that your children want to kill you. It can be easy to give in to those dark thoughts and start believing that your wee ones spend their days and nights scheming up ways to drive you insane, and thereby kill you from sheer exasperation. But this is hardly ever the case. In fact, in all the years I've been doing this stuff I've never come across a toddler who wanted to kill his or her mum or dad. The problem is that children have an exasperating tendency to act like ... well ... children. You have to keep reminding yourself that they've been on the planet for fewer years than you have fingers on one hand, and that they have an enormous amount to learn. Just getting their heads around walking, talking, and bowel control is quite a lot to do before they're five, let alone sorting out the pros and cons of good behaviour, and learning how to be a responsible member of the household. Some adults are still struggling with that stuff.

So always keep in mind that they haven't been here very long, and that their little brains are only just beginning to wrap themselves around the world. You can't really expect them to show a huge amount of maturity and wisdom; if you expect pettiness and silliness, you'll be far less disappointed. To remind myself of this very important point I have a conversation I often revisit with my boys when I feel in danger of forgetting it:

'Why do you always act like an eight-year-old?' I say to my youngest.

'Because I *am* eight,' he replies, slightly indignant.

'Ohhhh, yeah.'

Remember that life is suffering This is a Buddhist thing. Essentially Buddha said, some 2500 years ago now, that we often make ourselves unhappy because we expect life to be comfortable, and easy, and generally better than it usually is. The problem is, of course, that life is imperfect, and it often contains long stretches of unpleasantness. This is doubly true of parenting. It's fantastic, and amazing, and the greatest adventure you will ever have, but sometimes it really sucks.

It can be boring, and frustrating, and generally stressful. And those are just the good days.

If you expect the process of raising kids to be this grand sparkling adventure all the time, you'll feel a bit let down, and that will lead to feeling bitter, and then getting grumpy, and then angry, and then your head will explode and you'll die.

If you understand that we all experience these patches of grinding boredom, stress, frustration, and general misgiving, then it makes the whole thing somehow easier to bear. If you stop struggling against the current all the time by trying to make your family life something it can never be (or at least something it can only be for brief, fleeting, wonderful moments), then you can relax a little and deal with life as it is. Live where you are is my advice, not in some *Brady Bunch*-like fantasy. None of us has it easy, and that's simply part of the price you have to pay if you want to go on the ride. Once you get your head around this, the journey becomes considerably easier.

And when the pounding finally subsides — and it will — fix a slightly desperate smile on your face and get back out there. You have no choice, because it's bad form to hide in the bathroom for their entire childhood. Hiding in the bathroom for their *whole* childhood is cheating; a little hiding from time to time is OK ... just keep it in proportion is all I'm saying.

So fix that smile to your face with sticky-tape, and get back out there.

It happens to us all, make no mistake.

Your most important goal should be to get through the moment without your brain exploding. Then all you have to do is get through the next 20 or so years, and you should be fine. Simple, really.

To be on the safe side, though, it does pay to make sure the life insurance is all paid up. It's always important to have a Plan B.

3
Beware experts

Here's a paradox for you, a big 'un. This is a little book for parents — advice, wisdom, wit and the like — and one of the most important things I have to tell you is this: *Beware experts who write parenting books*. It's a strange paradox, true, but one I seem to be trapped in with no hope of rescue. You see, I really do think that all these experts telling people how to raise children is a problem, maybe even the single biggest problem that parents face. There's a constant cacophony of people telling us that if we don't raise our kids this way, or if we don't raise them that way, then we are failing them, or even condemning them to various unimaginable fates.

And my answer? What do I do in response? I write a bunch of parenting books and make a bunch of television shows about raising kids.

Why would I do that? Well, basically because it's the easiest way to tell as many people as I can that parenting isn't half as hard as the modern parenting movement would have you believe. Of course, sometimes when I say things like that I get accused of inventing the 'paper tiger' beige brigade. 'You've just made that lot up,' people have said.

You think? Well, think again. Over the past couple of years I've received a number of interesting emails/complaints/links to blogs where all manner of people have said all manner of things in this regard. For example, I received an email from the natural toilet-training league who said that they were disappointed that I had talked about nappies. In their view, nappies shame children (by strapping little bags of poo to their little selves) and should be done away with completely. Their view is that it's better to let children roam free, dropping their little jobbies where they will, and learning in their own sweet, pungent good time to poo in the right place. That way we avoid all the damaging shame and grow better children. Which is all fine and well if you have wooden floors, but if you have carpets then I can see one or two problems with this strategy. Stains being just one.

Now I don't have any issue with natural toilet-training. If you believe that it's better for your children to roam free and poo free as well, that's just fine with me. Everyone is entitled to see the world in whatever way works for them. What I don't like is when they tell you that, if you raise your children in a way they don't agree with, you are somehow harming or failing your children. These kinds of statements are almost always based on nothing more than their own weird theories, or on a distortion or spin on real science.

You see, I like science. It can tell us useful things about how the world works. It can be a handy compass when you're trying to find your way. Although it won't ever be more than a compass: because a compass can't tell you the best place to put your foot, but it can tell you which direction is north.

The problem is that a lot of the 'science' that gets talked about in the realm of parenting isn't science, or is bad science, or is good science that's been wildly exaggerated, twisted, or just plain fumbled. The people who write this stuff in books rely on the fact that normal people don't go rushing off to science libraries to check the 'facts' they state so boldly. Things like 'girls have more sensitive hearing than boys' (they don't), or 'boys' brains develop slower than girls' brains so they should start school a year later' (also not true). Who has the time to go look up journal articles to check that the 'expert' has got his or her facts straight? No one.

So don't automatically believe that, just because it's in a book or on TV, it's true. It might be, but it might not be as well. I include myself in this warning. Don't believe what I say just because I say it. I try to make sure I'm talking about the science stuff accurately, but unless you can verify it yourself then don't automatically trust me.

Bottom line: beware anyone who says if you don't raise your children their way then you will be damaging them.

Beware them most of all.

4
Relax:
we all mess it up

Don't worry too much about getting it right all the time, because you won't. Conversely, don't fret too much when you get it wrong, because you will — lots.

One night, hoarse from yelling, I sat beside my dear sweet little boy's bed and calmly informed him that if he really didn't want to live with us I would be happy to pack him a bag and walk down the street with him looking for a new family. It had been a bad night in our house, some might say completely mental. All of us had lost our respective rags at various points in the evening.

I wasn't bluffing.

I meant it.

The look on his little face when I put this proposition to him made it clear that he knew I meant it as well. He said that he didn't want to get a new family and that he would be a good boy and go to sleep. He kept his word, so we kept him. No bags were packed that night, or any other night since then, and we all still share the same postal address.

Now, here's the thing. As I was saying that to him, the little psychologist's voice up the back of my mind was telling me, in that very irritating measured tone it uses, that this was not an example of good parenting; in fact, quite the opposite.

You're just angry, said the painfully smug, know-it-all little voice. *He's just a child, and threatening to abandon him will likely cause deep-seated trauma.*

'Is that right?' the me-parent part of my brain replied.

Yes. It is. Shall we look at some more appropriate strategies?

'Well, actually,' the me-parent said, 'how about instead of doing that you just shut the hell up before I get the uncivilized parts of my brain to come over there and kick your arse?'

Is there any need for that kind of talk?

'Yes. There is.'

Oh.

And that was the end of that.

Sometimes we say and do things as parents that are less than shining. It would be great to think that that were not true, but it is. You want to minimize those moments as much as possible, but they are going to come. The trick is not to take them too lightly and not to take them too hard. You're human, so you're going to yell from time to time. There might even be — heaven forbid in these modern child-centred times — the occasional smacked bottom. You have to do as much as you can to make sure you aren't in that zone all the time, because that's no fun for anyone. If you live there *all* the time, then the kids will probably end up either robbing banks when they get older or spending all their spare change on shrinks, or worse still robbing banks so they can afford to spend it all on the shrinks.

That scenario aside, most of us are usually crap a small amount of the time, average for a big chunk in the middle, and really shine in scattered, memorable patches. This is the stuff of parenting. We have to survive them, and they have to survive us. That's how the game works. In the end we all learn about ourselves, both the good and the bad, and we learn either we can accept those things or we can't. The countless family gatherings that happen all over the world every day are a testament to both the genetic glue that holds us together and the forgiveness that allows a bunch of people with a sometimes rich and troubled history to come together in Northern Minnesota, or Madrid, or Buenos Aires, or Florence, or Blackpool or Dunedin, or a sheep station in the outback to celebrate Aunt Myrtle's 70th birthday or Cousin Matilda's wedding.

We all mess it up, but somehow most of us still manage to get to Aunt Myrtle's birthday in the end. Most of us will also probably be there for her funeral as well, which is good because Aunt Myrtle probably has a few bucks stashed away somewhere. It's as much about inheritances as it is about love.

5
Things they don't tell you: the bath poo

One of the many, many things no one ever tells you about before you have children is the bath poo. You don't imagine such things could be. You don't even stop to consider it. Let me tell you, though, that the bath poo is not a myth. It's real.

There is a particular facial expression that all parents of young children recognize. It's somewhere between a slightly horrified grimace and a curiously expectant smile, and it's the face they make just before they drop a wee log. That look comes only when the proverbial turtle is breathing fresh air, and it's the point of no return, because once the turtle gets a taste of freedom there's no going back.

The worst possible time that you can see that expression is when your little one is standing knee-deep in the bath. When you see that face, you know instantly what's coming. You freeze. Everything locks up. Curiously, you will also feel your own buttocks tighten, in some vain, cosmic attempt to stop what is happening. It is pointless, of course, because no amount of buttock-clenching on your part can stop the train of events that has been set in motion ... so to speak.

Then comes the panic, and closely following that is the lunging.

This is a very bad thing to do, because the little person,

terrified by your panic-stricken face and all the lunging, squeezes their little cheeks together in a reflex action. It is this squeezing which forces the half-emerged poo to separate like some kind of small, brown escape-capsule.

You watch it fall, and fall, and fall. *Plop.*

And there it is. A poo. In the bath. In *your* bath.

You watch it slide along the floor of the bath, not really registering what you're seeing. You know what it is, but your brain doesn't want to admit it. Then, as you watch, you suddenly realize that poo is soluble. You realize that poo dissolves in water. The reason you realize this is that small pieces of the poo detach from the main body and spread out along the floor of the bath.

And as you're watching all this — panic-stricken, half-lunged — you hear them. *Plop, plop, plop.*

Because, of course, it was never going to be just the one. Poo *always* travels in herds.

Then you really do lunge. You grab your little one, who is by now utterly confused and terrified by your reaction, and pull them from the bath. You hold them like that, dripping all kinds of stuff, dripping things you don't even want to consider.

At this point you call for help. You call for reinforcements. If you are a single parent, you will still call, although sadly no one will come. If you are part of a team, your other half will come. At this point they usually take the child, and then, almost always, they laugh. It is not funny for you, though, because you have to clean it up.

This is the point where you have to make a judgement call: do you pull the plug and pray, or do you scoop first? It's a tough call, because if you de-plug and it's too solid it'll wedge. If you try to scoop and it's too runny, then you'll probably vomit.

Besides, how exactly does one scoop a poo from a bath? It's not as though you have the tools to do a job like that just lying around. At this point, most of us go for the double-bag technique. Put your hand inside a plastic shopping bag, and then inside another one in case of leaks. Actually, it doesn't matter how many bags you use: there will always be a leak.

As you scoop someone else's runny poo from the bath, you wonder how your life ever became this horror, up to your elbow in a big, warm toilet. Ah well, you console yourself, at least it can't get any worse than this. At least now I've reached the grossest, lowest ebb of parenting. It can only get better from here. Yeah, right.

6
Ghosts make our cups of tea

One of the most important things you have to understand about being a parent, particularly if you want to stand the best chance of not screwing the whole thing up, and staying relatively sane, is that ghosts make our cups of tea.

We all take our tea a certain way. Some have milk, some don't. One sugar, two, three. Some — and clearly these are the more enlightened amongst us — don't take tea at all, preferring coffee. Those of us in premature training for the bed in the old people's home drink just a plain cup of hot water, thank you, dear, and some even drink those awful herbal teas which look like lawn clippings and taste, oddly enough, like scented lawn clippings.

Now each to their own, and whether your brew of choice be tea, coffee or scented lawn clippings, I'll wager that, for many of us, ghosts have a hand in what we drink.

Let me explain. Genes aren't the only thing we inherit from our parents; we also inherit our taste in hot drinks. A large number of us drink our tea (or coffee) the way our parents did. I, for instance, take my coffee white with one, as did my mum and dad. My wife takes her tea white with two, as did her parents. Over the years I have asked this question of a number of people, and by far the great majority of them take their tea (or coffee) the way their parents did. Now I'm not for a moment saying this is rigorous science. In fact it's so far away from anything resembling science that you should treat it simply as a fairly loose anecdote. That said, it's just something I've noticed as I've been wandering through life making various people cups of tea.

The point I'm trying to make is that we pick up all kinds of things from our parents, not just the colour of our hair and the length of our toes, but also all kinds of things that make us who we are. As a teenager I knew without a doubt that I was nothing like my own parents. There was nothing about me that was of them. In fact I was sure that I must be some kind of genetic anomaly, having inherited not a single jot that was theirs. (I was, in all truth, a fairly obnoxious teenager.) With the benefit of a few more years, and two kids, I have discovered more each day that I am my father, and my mother too. I find their voices coming out of my mouth at odd times, and this is both surprising and kind of nice at the same time. There is nothing better than knowing where you are from, and liking that place at the same time.

We are all from someone, that's how it works, and they are in our genes, and our minds, and our hearts. If you came from nice people and a nice place, then that is a comforting thought; but not all of us have. Some of us grew up in places that were cold, or frightening, and sometimes just plain nightmarish. Some of us knew horrors when we were little. What hope for these people?

Well, actually, there's plenty.

Sometimes you learn more about being a good parent

from having rat-shit ones. I have seen people who grew up in a nightmare who turned that around completely when they had kids of their own. I've seen people who came from the bleakest beginnings build wonderful families. We don't choose the families we come from, but we *do* get to choose the ones we make.

You can't do what your parents did just because it worked for you, and you also can't do the opposite because you didn't like what your folks did. Your parents aren't raising your kids: *you* are. *You* have to do what *your* kids need. You have to be clear about *what* you're doing and *why*. You have to pay attention to what's happening *now*, not when you were little.

The trick — and isn't there always a trick — is understanding when the *ghosts* are making the tea, and when *you* are. We learn all kinds of things from the people who raised us (or didn't raise us, as the case may be) and you have to know whose voice you're using.

So the next time you have a cup of tea, check to see who's making it. Is it you ... or is it the ghosts?

7
Tiny brains, ridiculous numbers

Whichever way you look at it, a trillion is a ridiculous number. Written in ones and zeros it is this:

$$1\ 000\ 000\ 000\ 000\ 000\ 000.$$

That's just silly. It's not really a number; it's more like a little row of caterpillar droppings. Yet, astoundingly, children's brains are made up almost entirely of ridiculous numbers just like this.

For example, your average newborn baby has approximately 100 billion brain cells (or neurons) at birth, which is about half the number it had as a foetus. The reason for the loss is probably based on the logic that it's good to have a 100 billion or so spare in case you drop some on the way. It isn't just the number of brain cells that is important, however; it's also the number of connections between these cells. It is the connections that allow information to flow in the form of 'impulses' which travel from neuron to neuron. Flow is good, very good in fact. Brains, like life itself, are all about connections.

But here's where it gets utterly ridiculous, because the average three-year-old has 1000 trillion connections going on, or 1 000 000 000 000 000 000 000 written in caterpillar faeces. This is about *twice* that of an adult, and is obviously just plain silly. This number is so big it doesn't make any kind of normal sense. One does not often go out and purchase 1000 trillion rolls of toilet paper or count even a single trillion shoelaces let alone 1000 trillion. Most of us will never do anything, of any description, by the trillion. Donald Trump probably does all the time, but the rest of us tend to work with smaller numbers. This said, clearly we can grasp the concept that we're talking about a lot of wiring and soldering iron here.

The reason they have more than us is not because they're smarter, but rather that they have a lot of disconnected bits hanging out of walls waiting for something to do. Over the course of their lives they connect up the ends to something useful, so that, hopefully, all the lights will eventually work exactly as they should. The other spare 500 trillion or so are simply binned.

There are two major implications from all this for us. The first is that we need to understand that children need to ask endless questions. If you have 1000 trillion connections in your head, you need to make some kind of use out of them. They have to figure out everything from gravity to spider webs as quickly as possible, so they're going to need to ask a few questions. They don't do it to make us crazy, they do it because they start off knowing basically nothing and have quite a bit of catching up to do.

The second is that it is a good thing to help them connect up the wires in as useful a way as possible. This doesn't mean you need to spend endless hours using flashcards and teaching them to spell their name by age two. That is simply being anal. The most important stuff is to be as stable, warm, and consistent as you can, and to let them play and explore their little world. It really is as simple as that. Humans evolved long before flashcards and reading programmes, so it's a safe bet that these things aren't essential for survival. All you pretty much need to do is feed 'em, water 'em, be nice, and brains basically wire themselves.

8
Little lips sink ships

I was once asked by a mum how she could stop her four-year-old from talking about private family matters at kindy. 'Easy,' I said, 'don't tell him.' It seems kind of obvious really. If you don't want the world to know something, then don't tell a pre-schooler, because they make blabbermouths look like shy introverts. Having said this, most people have quite a lot of complicated stuff going on in their lives and need to share at least some of that with their kids. Then the question becomes how much information is too much information — and working out the answer to that can be vexing. Parents are constantly having to make decisions about 'what we tell the kids' about all sorts of things from little issues to big ones.

The problem with kids is that they're naturally inquisitive, and they are also about as good at keeping secrets as drunken ex-spies who've just been made redundant because of funding cutbacks. In short, they always talk. As we've learned — unlike recently redundant ex-spies, who probably know more about the world than most people — with children the blabbing is because they actually understand so little about the world and are busy making those all-important connections in their tiny little brains. Further confounding things is that kids are both easily freaked out, and incredibly gullible. They really do believe just about any mad old thing you tell them. As a completely glaring 'for instance', they actually believe that a big lady dressed in a fairy costume comes and takes away their dead teeth. What's more, they think the creepy lady prowling about the house when they're asleep is exciting.

And as if all that weren't enough, there's also the completely reasonable-sounding modern parenting maxim that it's important to be honest with your children at all times. So parents should make sure their children understand what's happening all of the time, and why. It sounds great; after all, isn't honesty always the best policy?

Not really.

Honesty is a good thing, generally, but in my view it's wise to make sure it's dished out in ways that make sense to the particular age and stage that little people are at. I don't think you should always be completely honest with your children. In fact, I think quite the opposite. The adult world doesn't work on a full-disclosure policy, not by a long shot. The closest we ever come to full disclosure is with our partners, and even then a lot of the completely mad stuff we keep to ourselves. Truth be told, if we all knew everything about each other then I think civilization wouldn't be able to stand the strain of all that honesty.

Our governments certainly don't tell us everything. There's loads of stuff those guys keep from the rest of us. Some of that is for very good reasons, and some of that is for very self-interested reasons. Who knows, there might be aliens in some secret bunker in Area 51, and there might even be a bit of paper somewhere that has the name of the person who really shot JFK. Chances are that we'll never know because the people in charge of the world just don't want us to know some stuff. For the record, though, the only thing I personally think the US government has locked away in Area 51 is some old cheese sandwiches.

So if you, like me, believe that it isn't necessarily good for kids to know every last little thing that's going on, the question naturally arises as to where and how you draw the line. Asking yourself the three following questions might help you to decide what they need to know, and what they don't.

Do they really need to know?   Kind of obvious really, I know, but it's a good one to specifically think about. Mostly, little kids need a sense of security and stability. They need to know that the world is a fairly dependable place where the people in charge (Mum and Dad) have a pretty good handle on things. If you believe in the Tooth Fairy, monsters under the bed, and the big scary fat bloke in the red suit, then you need to have a pretty strong level of faith in the people in charge. At three it's confusing enough dealing with the stuff you can understand and control (which isn't much) without having your eyes opened to whole new areas of confusion and chaos. There are some things you do need to know, for sure, but not everything.

How will it help them to know?   Generally the reason you want to tell children things is because the information will help them. Usually it will either help them understand something that is confusing or unsettling, or prepare them for a change that is coming. For instance, it helps to know that we might be moving to a new house soon, but it does not help to know that the reason for this is that Mum has lost her job and so the bank is going to take our current house away. The golden rule here is: if you give them information, it should *relieve* them of some burden, not *add* to it.

How should I tell them? First and most important, pitch it at a level they can understand. The younger they are, the simpler the explanation. In reality, though, with very young children it's sometimes best to dodge the issue entirely and just make something up. For example, a few years ago we moved cities. This was particularly difficult for my oldest son, who was only four at the time. In the middle of all this his goldfish died. We could have explained to him that Goldy was now in heaven with Monty (our old cat), but in the end we decided that he had enough on his plate already, so we simply got another fish. Sometimes it's best to tell them the truth, and sometimes it's best to just get rid of the body and get another fish.

9
What kind of car is your kid driving?

It has long been my observation that we hit the ground with much of our personality already in place. Some remodelling happens along the way, but the basic machinery is there from the start. Our life experience definitely affects us, but even that effect is filtered through our personality. Some of us see the glass as half-empty, and some don't give a rat's arse about the glass and drink straight from the tap. We don't buy the car after we're born: we start off in the driver's seat from the get-go. So if we don't get to choose what kind of car we're driving, we need to learn how to make the most of the one that we've got.

A few years ago my good friend Ian Lambie and I celebrated the completion of his PhD by hiring a rental car and driving up a mountain. This might not seem that amazing, but then you had to see the road/goat track to understand what an achievement it was getting the car to the top. It was rugged, to say the least. In places, water had washed down the hills and left a jagged valley of huge boulders that looked impassable even to donkeys. We had a normal old sedan. Not a four-wheel-drive, not even a utility-type vehicle. We had a four-door family sedan.

At various points, the crossings looked so marginal that we stopped, got out, walked around, looked at angles, debated routes, estimated how much of the bottom of the car the boulders would rip out, and then had a go at getting through. It was so stressful we took turns driving. There was much grinding of metal and rock. We made it all the way up, and, just as amazingly, all the way down. There was damage (one particularly alarming piece of metal dragged along the road all the way home), but we made it. Even now I cannot believe that we managed to get a city car all the way up that seemingly impassable goat track of rock and mud. We pushed it to the edge and we lived to tell the tale.

Yet even as reckless and stupid as we were, we didn't take the car down the other side of the mountain, which had been the original plan. We were aiming for the traverse, but it was obvious that if we had taken it down the far side it would have slid off the track and down the cliff face. We had no food with us, and in that eventuality one would have had to have eaten the other. I'd like to think Ian would have volunteered because he was taller and thus had more meat on him than I did. Still, you can never tell about people. Friendships are only truly tested when someone has to get eaten.

The point being that, even though we pushed it to the edge — and indeed teetered slightly over the edge at several points — we knew there were limits. You have to know the limits of the car you're driving and adjust your plan accordingly.

Our job as parents is just the same. We have to teach our kids to understand what kind of car they're driving, and make the most of it. There's no point trying to get a four-wheel-drive kid to win on the Formula One Grand Prix circuit. It won't happen. But that same kid can get to places that the Formula One kids can only gaze at from a distance.

If your kid is a zippy little two-seater convertible, you need to teach them how to enjoy the sun, but also to anticipate the rain so they can stop and get the top up.

People-mover kids need to learn not to go too fast around corners, and also how to make sure everyone pays their share, because if you're the kind of kid with skills to move people places, then you're going to get free-loaders.

If your kid drives a tank, then they need to understand that that kind of power can be hugely effective, but can also scare the crap out of people. You can also sometimes run over your own guys, because it's sometimes hard to see what's in front of you. Don't always rush in, is what you teach tank kids; lay up a bit first and scout out the best approach. Most of all, try not to squash your own guys.

Find out what kind of car your kid is driving and then help them to make the most of that. Anticipate what their difficulties might be, and teach them the skills to navigate their way through. Build on strengths and figure out the weaknesses.

Success — however your kids eventually define it — is all about knowing how to get there without crashing.

10
Toddlers, dawdling, and little stoned hippies

Here's the thing: even when I'm not in a hurry, if I end up driving behind someone doing 40 kilometres an hour in a 50 kilometres an hour zone, I experience an almost overwhelming sense that I am in fact in a tremendous hurry. What's more, the longer I have to follow this slow-poke, the greater my sense of urgency becomes, and the more frustrated I feel that this inconsiderate nincompoop in front of me is now personally responsible for the fact that I will now be late, even though I don't actually have anywhere in particular to be. I don't think I'm the only one who experiences this. I think many people do. There is something tremendously frustrating about people going slow.

I don't like to muck around. I like to get in, do what you have to do, and get out. I'm not fun to shop with. I don't want to browse. 'Find, buy, leave' is my motto. I do not want to dally. I found antenatal classes frustrating because everything was said five times. Say it once and then we can all get home early was what I thought.

All of which is why toddlers have been a great trial for me.

Toddlers are the biggest dilly-dallyers this side of the black stump. Toddlers do not know the meaning of the word 'focused'; at least they do not know what the word means in relation to anything I'm remotely interested in, such as getting out the door on time. They are able to focus on any one of a number of irrelevant and frivolous details.

For instance, they are able to focus on how bendy the strap of their sandal might be, yet show little concern for the fact that we are already fifteen minutes late to meet our friends for a coffee. They are also able to focus on making a block tower stand up at a slightly wonky angle, but at the same time have scant regard for the fact that if they aren't in bed in the next three minutes I will miss the start of *American Idol* (and, what's more, it's the initial auditions where all the crazy people try out and fail).

While there are many times during the wondrous experience that is parenting when I feel my head will explode from sheer frustration, it is the dillying and the dallying which have brought me closest to death by cerebral combustion. One can only feel sympathy for snail mums and dads, because the very idea of having to parent a dawdling young snail seems incomprehensible.

The thing is, young children exist mainly in the here and now — a condition Buddhists call 'mindfulness', and something they train for years to perfect. Little kids don't have to train; they're naturals. Life will teach them to get all hung up on what happened before and what might be going to happen next, but at the beginning they are masters of mindfulness. They don't have much concept of the future, and they don't tend to hang on to the past. Their hearts may break in one moment when the block tower collapses yet again, but they are able to let go of the pain and move forward with relative ease. We might carry the resentment around with us, but little kids are not burdened with these kinds of attachments — they move on, unencumbered by their pasts. Sounds kind of nice, doesn't it?

The other thing is that, because they operate in the here and now, they experience the world far differently to us. They literally become lost in the detail. For the little mind the world is full of miracles, all the way from monkey tails to toe nails. Everything is new, and wondrous, and exciting. They have no preconceived notions about toe nails, and so they approach each new toe nail they find with an open and inquiring mind. They want to experience the toe nail in the most profound way possible. Yeah, baby.

All of which sounds a little like a 1960s LSD trip, and in many ways it is. So the easiest way to cope with toddlers dawdling is to realize that effectively you're trying to organize and manage a little stoned hippy. When you think about it like that, it all starts to make a lot more sense.

You can't expect them not to dawdle or get distracted, any more than you could expect a little stoned hippy not to listen to Jimi Hendrix, but there are some ways to make it a little easier:

1. Leave enough time. Don't expect them to be able to rush around at the last minute, because they can't. Give yourself plenty of time.

2. Get their attention. Remember they are easily distracted, so make sure they have actually heard you.

3. Reduce distractions and background noise. Turn off televisions, music, and the like. Take books and little bits of Lego out of little hands.

4. One thing at a time. Don't give them six orders at one go — just take it one step at a time. For example, instead of saying 'Get your sandals on' you could first say 'Find your sandals', then 'Sit down on the mat', then 'Put on the sandal in your hand', then 'Put the other one on'.

5. If they are a little older, use the microwave timer to help them stay focused.

6. Even though it probably doesn't even need to be said, praise them for each step in the right direction.

The main things to remember are that it's normal for them to dawdle, and it's normal for you to feel wound up about it. Try to remain calm as much as you can, because once the yelling starts it all usually ends in tears. Give yourself plenty of time and give them simple one-step instructions.

Sometimes, despite your best-laid plans it will all go haywire and you'll end up being terribly late for something terribly important. When that happens, try to keep a little perspective on things. As a friend of mine helpfully points out from time to time whenever I get worked up about something, in a hundred years we'll all be dust and none of this will matter anyway.

The other thing is that when you do have time, and perhaps also a coffee, let them dawdle to their little heart's content. This is how they learn about the world and its wonders, so, when you have the time and the inclination, maybe indulge their need to poke about in stuff. It can be tremendous fun to spend time with a little stoned hippy.

11

All they want is to rule the world

Once you understand that all kids want is to rule the world, you'll be fine. They don't want much, just total world domination, which is of course completely mad. It's not their fault, that's just the way children are. Some of them grow out of it, some of them become evil criminal geniuses, some become parking wardens, and some become President.

The point is that you have to understand their ultimate goal (ie, total world domination) before you can understand their behaviour. This is why little people react with such outrage when their block tower falls over, since gravity too is supposed to be under their dominion. They want the blocks to lean at a ridiculous angle and not fall. Why should gravity have to apply to *them*? This is also why they become so incensed when you do not pander to their every whim, because in their little megalomaniacal minds their whim is the only whim worth pandering to. You don't get to have a whim, because you're not the boss of everything. They, on the other hand, are.

Where you come unstuck is if you don't correct this belief. If you let little Tarquin or Portia continue with this belief in their own omnipotence, then it will not end well. They will begin by having tantrums over block towers, then progress to making trips to the supermarket nightmarishly unbearable, and it will end with you having to call the police because your teenage hoodlum child is smashing up the house. Believe me, I've seen it.

It is reasonable and normal for our little ones to want to rule the world. It's our job to teach them that they can't. If we don't, then they will run your world, and they will more than likely make it a misery. It's far easier to depose a two-year-old dictator than a 22-year-old one.

12
Mums

Mums are great, but they can also be a pain in the arse. Mums are fantastic at things like making sure the kids get fed with healthy stuff, that raincoats are packed, that underwear is clean, and that teeth are properly brushed. Mums also know when temperatures are raised, where favourite toys are kept, and what clothes go with the red shoes. Mums know their kids' friends' names, and their kids' friends' mums' names. Mums know how to make morning teas that are wholesome, warm, and freshly baked. Mums can always find the keys, unless someone else has shifted them.

There are countless things mums are good at.

Mums also worry about stuff. They sometimes make a bit of a fuss over things that aren't that big a deal. Mums take the view that homework should always be done and that hands must always be washed before eating. Mums are less likely to let you eat stuff that's fallen on the ground.

Mums disagree with statements like 'No one ever died from going to the supermarket in bare feet.' What's more they can often produce case studies to prove it isn't so.

Mums, as a general rule, are less likely to let you climb stuff. Mums think more about gravity, and specifically about what happens when gravity and a lack of climbing skills collide. Mums think that danger is a bad thing. Mums worry about losing an eye.

Mums ask a lot of questions. Lots, and lots, and lots of questions.

Mums think it's a myth that no one ever died of scurvy in this country from not eating their vegetables. Mums think scurvy is a major health concern afflicting many families.

Mums always know where you are, even when you don't want them to.

All these things are what make mums so great.

13
Dads

Dads are great, but they can also be completely bloody hopeless. Dads are great because they let you climb dangerous sharp things. Dads let you steer the car up the drive. Dads know that if it doesn't involve some kind of danger then it's just not as much fun. Dads buy you more junk food. Dads will not only let you eat stuff that's dropped on the ground, they'll actively encourage it. Dads can fart, burp, and swear. Dads can chuck you up in the air so high you hit your head on the ceiling. Dads can hang you upside-down 'til you feel like your head is going to burst.

Dads are cool.

Dads can also be pretty hopeless. They sometimes forget to give you morning tea because they're watching sport on the telly. When they do make morning tea, it tends to be whatever they can grab from the cupboard that requires no more preparation than unwrapping. Dads forget to take hats, gloves, and coats, and if they do take them they are more likely to lose these items. Dads often won't lose a pair of gloves, they just lose the left one.

Dads sometimes take a while to notice that you're sick.

Dads sometimes overdo it and scare the willies out of little kids by chucking them up so high they bang their head on the ceiling.

Dads sometimes take things way too personally at sports matches.

Dads are sometimes too busy to notice that you're bored, hungry, or not there.

Dads, as a general rule, have no conception of how to brush your hair in a way that doesn't make you look a doofus. Dads have no idea which clothes are 'good' clothes and which ones are 'everyday' clothes. Dads have great difficulty dressing children in clothes that 'go', full stop. Dads think that if it fits, even marginally, then it goes.

Dads have an amazing ability to lose kids whenever they are left in sole charge.

All this stuff is why dads are so cool.

14
They probably won't lose an eye

We worry terribly for our children. No one tells you this, but when they give you the baby you also get two buckets: one full of worry, and one full of guilt. One of the things we worry about is the ever-present danger of losing an eye. For some primal reason this thought fills most parents with dread. You don't often hear parents warning children that if they aren't careful they'll lose an ear, but we hear an awful lot about eyes.

Let me tell you a story that might help.

I was in the park with my then three-year-old son on his bike, trying to teach him how to brake. He wasn't getting it.

'Pedal backwards,' I said, endlessly, but he wasn't making the connection.

At one point he started to roll down a gentle incline towards a bamboo bush. He wasn't going that fast, and bamboo is quite flexible, so I made the decision to let him have a wee crash to reinforce the point that a lack of braking is generally a bad thing.

What I was not aware of was that a shaft of bamboo had broken off, handily exactly at three-year-old eye-height, and was angled right at my now wide-eyed-with-fear son heading towards the bush at a gentle speed. Now, the interesting thing about bamboo is that when it breaks, rather than a single jagged spike, the broken end has what can only be described as a whole bunch of incredibly sharp needles poking straight up.

At this point, when I tell this story to an audience, there are always two very distinct reactions: the mothers in the audience cover their faces in horrified anticipation, and the dads look curious to see how this one turns out.

So my boy hits the bush as I saunter along, three metres or so behind, thinking smugly that he has just learned some quality lessons from the school of hard knocks. There was a pause, and then he started to howl. It was not a 'wow that was scary' howl, or a 'look at me, look at me' howl; no, this was a 'my head has just been ripped open' howl.

This was a no-bullshit howl.

I knew straight away that, whatever happened, I was likely going to be in serious trouble with his mother.

I rushed up and he turned to me, still howling, and that's when I saw the blood. The jagged shaft had cut him all the way up his cheek, all the way up his lower right eyelid, all the way up his upper eyelid, and then further up his forehead. There was a lot of blood, and for a moment I thought I'd just made a pirate. Quite aside from his obvious distress, I knew that I was in for a bollocking from his mother. Then he opened his eyes to howl and I saw, miraculously, that they were both still there, and both still working.

Brilliant.

Looking at the wound, it was obvious that his eye must have retracted up inside his skull to have missed being punctured. I was happy, since this now meant that obviously children had excellent protective eye reflexes and I could be even less vigilant in the future. I chalked that one up as a point for the school of hard knocks.

So the moral of this story is that they probably *won't* lose an eye, which means we can all relax a bit more and let them crash into stuff a bit more, just like our parents did for us.

And if they do, well, glass eyes can be pretty cool, too, particularly if you get a zombie-undead glass eye to scare away the bullies.

That would be almost *worth* losing an eye for.

15
The power of punctuation

You might think that punctuation has very little to do with raising kids, but you'd be wrong. The effective use of punctuation is the most powerful parenting tool that you have. The rule of thumb is this: full stops are very good, commas are very bad, and question marks should be used sparingly. Men have an intuitive understanding of this rule; women, on the other hand, love commas and question marks as much as they love shoes.

For instance, this is how dads ask how their kid's day at school was:

> Dad: 'How was your day, son?'
> Kid: 'Alright, I guess.'
> Dad: 'Good.'

And that's it. All done. Six words, one question mark, one full stop.

Here's how mums ask about the day at school:

> Mum: 'How was your day, son?'
> Kid: 'Alright, I guess.'
> Mum: 'Who did you play with?'
> Kid: 'I dunno.'
> Mum: 'You must know who you played with?'

Kid: 'I dunno. James and Steven.'

Mum: *Pause.* 'Steven?'

Kid: *Sighs.* 'Yeah.'

Mum: 'Steven Jones?'

Kid: 'Yeah.'

Mum: 'Why are you playing with him? Is he the one who was on your soccer team last year? And you guys didn't get on? And his dad was yelling all the time at you guys to try harder? That one?'

Kid: *Sounding confused and irritated.* 'Yeah … no … ah whatever.'

Mum: 'There's no need to be rude, I'm just asking.'

And asking, and asking, and asking.

Or this example of how mums and dads tell kids off:

Dad: 'Stop being an idiot and pick up your clothes.'

Mum: 'Why can't you ever do what I ask? I spend all day cleaning up after you guys, picking up after you, taking your dirty dishes into the kitchen, vacuuming up crumbs, and you can't even pick up your clothes? What do I have to do to get the message through? I say it over, and over, and over, but no one seems to even care. I don't know why I bother most of the time. I should just leave this place and then we'd see what happens. It'd be a mess within a day, and there'd be no food in the house, and no clean clothes, and nothing else either …'

That's nine words versus 110 and still counting.

The single most common piece of advice that I give parents is to address their use of punctuation. Don't overuse the comma. In fact, don't use it at all if you can help it. Anything worth saying can be said without a comma. Whatever comes after the comma will just be nagging to them. Anything after the comma will simply cause resistance, ill-will, and more trouble. Most arguments can be drastically shortened with more judicious use of the full stop.

If you are saying anything to kids, then you need to make the rule that the first time you can use a full stop, you will.

The punctuation rules become even more critical as you move into adolescence, so best get practising now.

Full stop.

16
Not too loose, not too tight

Structure is good, very good in fact. Structure helps things to run smoothly. Structure gives kids a sense of what's coming so they can start to get themselves ready for what comes next. A good clear structure helps at all kinds of levels. It'll help you get through the day as much if not more than it helps them. The trick with structure is much the same as choosing underpants: not too loose, and not too tight.

Too loose, they slowly work their way down to the ground; too loose, you get cold.

Too tight makes life a slow-building misery; too tight will give you blisters.

Kids who grow up with no structure are not as happy, in my experience. Kids want and need rules and routines. When their days are regular and predictable, they can relax and get on with the business of being a kid without always having to work out what the hell is going on. It's kind of reassuring when you're a kid to know that the first thing you do when you get home from school is wash your hands, have a snack, and then watch *SpongeBob*. That's a nice little routine. That's something you can actually look forward to.

Kids who grow up with too much structure, on the other hand, become either accountants or serial killers, or sometimes both. If you have to get up on the dot of 7.30 a.m., brush your teeth 28 times top and bottom, dress in a prescribed order, and sit and wait in absolute silence until 8.35 a.m. when you depart for school by the front door walking at the designated pace, then you're probably going to end up killing people and burying them in the basement when you get older. You will also probably find yourself neatly cataloguing who is buried where.

Not too loose, people, not too tight.

17
When good kids go bad

They prepare you for many things at antenatal classes, far more things than you could ever have imagined you might need to know. I certainly think it would be fair to say that most dads learn far more than we ever want to know. I think dads would prefer that many of the things we learned at antenatal classes had remained a mystery. For example, before antenatal classes I had never heard of the term 'mucus plug'. If I had heard that term arise in conversation, I would have thought that it was a plumbing situation which required the use of a generously sized plunger.

Oddly, that is something close to the truth.

Equally oddly, or perhaps understandably, one of the things they do not tell you about is how angry your children will make you feel. Over the course of my career, as well as working with kids and families I have also spent a great deal of time working with criminals of all descriptions. I have sat in rooms with arsonists, and bank robbers, and gang members of all denominations and yet strangely the only two people on the face of the planet who have made me feel angry enough that I needed to go and have a lie down because of the pounding sensation in my brain are my own dear, sweet sons. I love them, don't get me wrong, but on occasion they have nearly killed me out of sheer unadulterated frustration.

It is a high-stakes game, this parenting lark, and the politics are complicated. Parents are, after all, occupying forces in their children's lives, and no occupying force in the history of the world has ever managed to hold on to power. Eventually, even if we try to hang on to them forever, they will overthrow us and establish their own government. Shortly after that, they will put us in a retirement home for old dictators where mean nurses will poke us with sticks. What is far more preferable, and indeed graceful, is a gradual transition from anarchy and lawlessness to stable independent government.

So how do we civilize these tiny barbarian hordes?

Build fences   If you don't put up some fences, you can't really complain. It's in the nature of children to roam, to explore, and to cause good-natured havoc. So it's a bit limp to complain about bad behaviour if you don't attend to the basics of fence-building. Fences are good for children because fences give them a way to start figuring out how the world works. The happiest kids are the ones who know what they are allowed to do and what they aren't allowed to do.

Put a guard on the wire   Once you've built your fence, make sure you keep monitoring it. Just as it's the nature of children to roam, it's also in their nature to try to find a way around any fences they find in their path. If no one is watching, they will simply slip through and then wreak havoc in all kinds of ways.

Make sure everyone knows where the fence is   In the spirit of fair play, make sure everyone is clear about where the fence-line is. There's no point in making a rule if no one knows what it is. By the same token, you can't keep shifting the fence-line either. If you dig in, then you need to stay dug in. The more you shift the lines, the more you encourage them to keep pushing.

Insurgency is to be expected   Occasionally there will be an outbreak of insurgency. This is only natural and to be expected. Don't get all angry and huffy about the whole thing and engage in some widespread crackdown: it's their job to push back, and it's our job to remind them that their time to rule has not yet come. It's also important not to give up whenever the bottles start flying. Sadly, we must stay the course, even though there are many times it might seem far easier just to get out. We started it, so we have to finish it.

Never negotiate with terrorists   While it's entirely natural for children to engage in acts of insurgency, it's important they understand that parents do not negotiate with terrorists. If you let them bully you into something, or you simply give in under a sustained assault (of any kind), then you are in big trouble. Children must learn that we'll not engage in any form of dialogue with terrorists. Terrorism will only result in immediate, measured, and carefully targeted reprisals. If they learn the government won't be held to ransom, they won't even bother starting it up.

Feed the good, starve the bad   As with all developing nations, different factions will arise. Some of them will be progressive, some not. We need to be careful to feed the factions we approve of, and starve the ones we do not. Now, because we're not the CIA, I'm not actually talking about starving children of food; instead we need to reward the good behaviour and ignore the bad stuff. Children, like all political factions, thrive on attention — so make sure you're paying the good guys.

Keep your word   There's no point making countless empty threats. You must be true to your word. If you say something is going to happen (for example, time out, early bedtime, loss of television time), you must follow through. If the little barbarians learn that your word counts for nothing, then you'll end up using many, many, many words and achieving less and less and less.

Model good government   Most of all, we must model good government. None of us is perfect to be sure, but we must try to act as we would want them to act. We won't always be able to manage that, because life is complicated and we all screw up from time to time, but we must try. They will look to us to see how business is done, and so we must offer the best example we can of how to govern. We must be as fair, and even, and measured as we can be. We must be forgiving, but we must not be weak. We must show them that getting along and working together beats conflict and struggling against.

And if all that fails, best have a helicopter at the embassy and leave it to the UN to clean up the mess.

Good luck.

18
Little hot-heads

You'd think that, for your average pre-schooler, there really isn't that much to get wound up about in life. They have it — let's be honest — pretty sweet. If you don't like something, you just spit it out. If you want something, anything, you just scream until someone brings it. If you're tired, no matter where you are, you just sleep. It doesn't matter if you're in bed, on the potty, in the car or on horseback, if you're tired you just nap right then and there without having to be concerned about falling off, getting home, the weather conditions, or if you drool and people are watching. You don't have to worry about taxes, the dishes, or whether there's enough petrol in the car to get you to your next meeting. You also, when push literally comes to shove, don't even need to worry about finding a toilet, because someone helpfully straps a purpose-built poo-catching device right there.

And yet still they do seem to get angry with alarming, and often wearying, regularity. So what's all that about?

Well, in life not everything goes your way, and you can't have everything you want. This revelation seems particularly upsetting for your average pre-schooler who begins with the belief that not only does the world owe them a living, but also that living needs to be delivered completely on their terms in a manner and timeframe of their choosing. Reality can only disappoint. So they get cranky. Three different factors are at work: temperament, development, and how we respond to their behaviour.

Temperament is a huge influence. We're each born with a particular temperament, and this temperament remains remarkably stable across our lives. While we develop and grow as people, the basic 'who we are' pretty much stays who we really are. If you're stubborn at three, then you'll probably be stubborn at 23 and 33 as well. We might mellow and modify our behaviour with age and experience, but the fundamentals of who we are remain unchanged.

For those of us with more than one child, there is usually an easy one and one who's a little more 'high maintenance'. In my experience, it has nothing to do with birth order, or gender, or anything else. You just tend to get an easy one, and one who's a bit harder. This usually becomes apparent when it comes to crankiness — some children are just naturally more cranky than others. They don't become cranky; they pretty much start out that way. Others seem to be just naturally mellow and happy little people. Whatever the case, there's an element of crankiness that's simply beyond our control, because that's just how each little person is wired together.

Development also plays a big role. In those early years, just as they must learn to walk, talk, and drop the wee brown jobbies in the big white seat, they must also learn to manage their emotions, including their frustration, disappointment, and general crankiness. We all get frustrated, disappointed, and cranky; it's just that after a while you figure out that falling on the floor and screaming really doesn't help things much. The reason pre-schoolers are notorious for tantrums is that their desire often far outstrips their actual ability. They want to climb onto the chair, but they simply can't reach it. They want to make the rain stop, but for some reason the clouds don't seem to be listening. They can see and reach and want a whole lot more with each passing day, but often their physical abilities simply aren't yet up to the job.

It's also important to remember that they believe the universe revolves around them. Even while they are starting to get their heads around the idea that other people may have different ideas to theirs, they're still working on the basic principle that if they see it, then it belongs to them, and that any stray whim they have must be immediately satisfied. Believing this means they're setting themselves up to be pretty frustrated and cranky a lot of the time.

Our responses are the third part of the equation. As the single biggest influence in their little lives, how we respond can have a significant impact on how long that black cloud of tiny outrage/fury hovers. Here's a few hints to keep you headed in the right direction — and hopefully keep you relatively sane.

→ Structure is good. Don't go crazy and map out every last second, just keep a rhythm to their day and they tend to be happier.
→ Sleep is important. We all get cranky when we're tired, so make sure they're getting enough and at the right times.

Learn your particular little one's warning signs that they're tired, and respond.

➡ Remember, 5–7 p.m. is awful for all of us. Just take a deep breath, dig in, and push through to the other end.

➡ Distraction is 90% of the battle. They have such tiny attention spans that distracting them can be enough to solve most cranky situations.

➡ Time out is your trump card. Sometimes they just completely melt down and there's nothing much you can do except put them somewhere quiet and safe and wait for the storm to pass. Reasoning with a tantruming three-year-old is not an option; time out it. What's more, once deprived of an audience, tantrums tend to sputter out after a while.

Storms in the pre-school years are normal. There's a lot going on in their bodies and brains, and a lot they have to work out in the world as well. So it's pretty reasonable that from time to time they're going to get a bit fed up and lose their little rags. Just remind yourself that they won't be screaming for the red cup when they're 26, then put them somewhere quiet for a bit until they calm down (when their cherub-like wee faces change from that angry mottled purple back to something more human-looking), make yourself a cup of tea, and reflect on what a constant joy it is to be a parent.

19
Bolshy toddlers — born to rule

There's also a thuggish element to most pre-schoolers. That same combo of frantic change and learning with limited skills — and being focused on the here and now — makes for the perfect fertilizer to feed the inner thug which lives inside them all.

So, a little basic thuggery is pretty normal, and nothing much to be alarmed about. The world might be obsessed with the idea that children should be nice all the time, but they sometimes have a different view. There's a thug in your midst. Sure, it's not nice when your wee Janine walks up to another child at pre-school and bowls them over with a well-placed shove, but this doesn't make her a fledgling criminal. Kids bopping kids is an unavoidable part of the journey from primitive pre-schooler to civilized adult. Imagine the sense of wonder your average toddler feels when he or she first discovers the joys of the simple shove. How great must that be? Now when people annoy you, with the careful placement of tiny hands and a bit of forward momentum you can shift the argument along significantly. What's more, you'll soon learn that the repertoire can be expanded out to punching, kicking, hair-pulling, pinching, and the old tried-and-tested simple-as-you-like slap.

If we were all a little more honest about these things, we

might admit that this urge to give the people who cross us a jolly good shove never completely disappears; we just get better at controlling it.

But sometimes a little pushy becomes a lot pushy, and suddenly you're getting 'that look' from the other mums at coffee group. What do you do then?

First off, take a look at your little one's temperament. As parents, we all know instinctively that our kids are born with a large amount of who they are hard-wired in place. Many mums report that their stubborn toddlers were stubborn in the womb as well, refusing to stop kicking if their mums were in a position that didn't seem to agree with them. Now, while I don't know if that's a fact beyond the anecdotal stories mums have told me, you can see temperament types from as early as age three, and they remain relatively constant through life.

We know this thanks to the tireless efforts of our friends at the Dunedin Multidisciplinary Health and Development Study at Otago University. For the past 38 years they have been following a group of more than 1000 people born in Dunedin between 1972 and 1973, and have discovered a whole host of things about what shapes us as human beings; including that around 28% of children had a 'confident' temperament style — bold little souls who weren't reluctant to blunder into things and impose their will on anyone who got in the way. They were loud, pushy, and supremely confident that their way was probably best, and that everyone else should probably just do what they were doing.

The good news is that at age 26 they tended to be outgoing, positive, go-getters. They wanted to take the world by the horns and continue to lead the way, just as they had when they were toddlers. All of which is well and good, but it doesn't make it any easier when it's your little one who always seems to be the one causing trouble, does it? So, what to do?

Many years ago when I worked at a child and family unit in Auckland, we had a saying about pushy little people: 'Strong-willed children require strong-willed parents.' Does this mean you have to engage in a head-on confrontation with your little person? No, it just means that you can't be a wet rag. You can't let your pre-schooler walk all over you, because that way lies anarchy. Instead, you have to get your head in the game and make sure that you are running things according to your plan, and not at the mercy of their whims. Here's how.

→ Model calmness. I say this with a not completely straight face, because I know parenting is a constant battle between the desire to stay calm and the urge to lose your rag and holler. We all holler, but at least try to keep things as calm as you can. It generally ends better that way.

→ Explain what you want in small steps with small words. Remember that a two-year-old has about the same language abilities as a chimpanzee, so keep it very simple and direct. Long-winded explanations muddle their little heads, so keep it simple, and clear.

→ Reward good behaviour. This is so basic it almost makes me cringe to write it, but it's true nonetheless. Their world is very small and you are a large part of it, so the more attention you give to good behaviour the 'gooder' they are likely to be.

➡ Punish bad behaviour. A lot of people don't like the 'p word', but the simple fact is punishment is how we learn. And it's hardly rocket science: if you do something and the consequence is unpleasant, you're less likely to do it again. For pushy pre-schoolers the punishments of choice are time out and giving stuff up. If you throw the block, you lose the blocks; if you hit your friend, you can't play with them for a few minutes ... until the wisdom of that particular course of action sinks in.

➡ At all times, remember that they are only tiny and there is still a huge amount of development to go. Be patient — they are only just learning how to be people, and they are bound to make a few mistakes along the way. Mistakes are how we learn.

The main thing to get your head around here is that pushiness is probably just a part of who they are. Evidence suggests they were born that way, so don't try to make them into someone they're not — simply harness what they are. Put some firm limits and boundaries around them, and help them to learn how to manage their personality. Oomph is good, as long as you can control it, and so the best thing you can do for these little ones is to learn how to do just that. As with almost everything else, it's firm, clear limits, praise the good, punish the bad. Just do that over and over for about 20 years and then it should all be fine.

20
Sleeping is like riding a bicycle

Let's be honest, they may look like angels when they're asleep, but really, who the hell cares? They're quiet, and they're still. They could look like mutant hillbilly freaks and we'd still be happy. If you're spending a lot of time watching your kids while they're asleep, then you're missing the point. The real point is that when they're asleep, you get to pretend you still have a life. You get a couple of hours where you get to play normal people.

Sleep is a treasure beyond measure. You need them to sleep or you will die, not physically, but psychologically. The you-who-was-before will simply die. Your body will shuffle through the motions, but inside you've already started to break down. You see this in the faces of people whose kids don't sleep. They are the walking dead. Not living, but not quite gone.

What a lot of people don't realize, however, is that sleep is a lot like riding a bicycle: both are acquired skills, and both usually end in tears if not done properly. If you're a lie-on-the-couch-and-bellow-at-the-kids-to-get-into-bed kind of parent, you might want to rethink that strategy. Think of it this way: if you lay on a couch down at the park and bellowed at the kids to 'ride that damn bike why don't ya', how well do you think that would work? Yelling does not a cyclist make. You need to start with trainer wheels and work your way up from there. You need someone to help you steer, and someone to stop you from crashing into stuff. (Although as we saw in *They probably won't lose an eye*, you maybe don't need to worry quite so much about this one.) Whatever the case, they're going to need some more help to learn how to ride a bike other than you lying around yelling.

It's the same with sleep. It's a skill. It won't just happen by itself. Left to their own devices, children will end up finally going to sleep on the roof of the neighbour's house at 3.00 a.m. Lying on the couch bellowing at kids to go to sleep is as pointless as lying on the grass yelling at them to take off the trainer wheels and not fall off all the damn time. It might feel easier, but it isn't going to work.

If you want them to sleep, you must teach them to sleep. You must have a good routine heading into sleep-time so they know what's coming. You must keep it as calm and quiet as you can. Dinner, bath, stories, bed. Get rid of all the silly stuff that gets in the way, like fruit drinks, strobe lights, karaoke, television, dancing bears. While there might well be an occasion where dancing bears are appropriate, it is not bedtime.

There is never a time for karaoke. Karaoke is wrong in every way.

Once you get them into bed, then you dig in. The only option at that point is sleep. Whenever they get up, you put them back, quietly and calmly, and you get out again. If you switch to autopilot, and simply channel them back into bed with no eye contact and no interaction, then they will sleep. The only way to learn to ride a bicycle is to get back on every time you fall off. If you decide that sleep is the only possible outcome, then it will come. If you don't, it won't. If you doubt, you'll still be there at midnight.

Always remember that sleep is a fundamentally important life skill, because if your kids don't learn the skills to sleep, well, then you will have no life.

21
Fine young cannibals

Did you know that rotten human brains taste like cheese? I do. I learned this fact in high school when I read the book *Alive* by Piers Paul Read.

Alive is the story of a team of football players from Uruguay who survived a plane crash in the Andes in October 1972. The really remarkable thing about this story, however, was not so much that these people survived in the Andes mountains for 72 days, but *how* they survived.

The problem they faced was that they didn't have anything to eat. They had shelter in the form of the wreckage of the plane, and they had water from melting snow. What they didn't have was food. They rationed the bits and pieces they'd managed to scavenge from the wreckage as best they could, and waited for help. Soon, though, the chocolate bars ran out and the rescuers never came. Finally, after some debate, they ate the bodies of their dead team-mates.

Fair enough. Who wouldn't? In the right context cannibalism seems perfectly sensible. In the middle of the suburbs it's plain creepy, but in the mountains it makes complete sense.

The moral of this story is that hungry people eat, and if they get hungry enough they'll even eat each other. This same principle applies to fixing the problem of little kids who won't eat. Basically it's simple: you just let them get hungry, then they'll eat.

If they only eat crap, stop serving them crap. Don't put the chips on the plate and they pretty much can't eat them.

If they won't eat the healthy meal you put in front of them, then take it away. Let them sleep on an empty stomach and watch them tuck in at breakfast time.

I guarantee that if all you had in the freezer were bits of Uruguayan footballers then sure your kids might turn their noses up at first, but give them a few days and they'd be tucking into a meaty thigh as if it were chicken.

Luckily, the same principle that applies to human flesh also applies to broccoli, carrots, and lettuce.

Hungry children eat — that's pretty much all you need to know.

22
The *real* Golden Rule

After all these years working with all kinds of kids and families, I think that managing behaviour boils down to one simple principle: Don't make their problem your problem.

Surely it can't be that simple? I hear you say.

Actually, I think it is.

To understand it, though, you need to think like an economist. Up until a few years ago I used to think that economics was just stuff that people who worked in banks were interested in. I thought economics was simply all about foreign exchange rates and inflationary pressures. To my great surprise I've since discovered that economics is just as relevant to raising kids as it is to raising interest rates.

Why? Because every day toddlers plot and plan corporate takeovers in their very own financial system. They are ruthless traders in the naughty economy, and like all Wall Street types they want to take over the world. They bargain hard for the best deal they can get with little concern for anyone but their shareholders.

A very simple economics drives behaviour in tiny folk, and all of us in fact, and it's this: How much does it cost? Before they decide to do something, they have to decide if the cost of the behaviour is worth the outcome. So, if you're three years old and you want to throw a block at the cat, you need to weigh up the costs and benefits of the behaviour. On the plus side it's kind of fun to throw stuff at the cat, because it's intensely interesting to explore what sort of effect blocks have on cats. Also the cat generally bolts out of the room, which, if you're a three-year-old megalomaniac, is very satisfying indeed. Finally, it gets you some quality one-on-one time with your mum or dad as they explain to you why we don't throw blocks at Fluffy. On the down side, you might get put in your room or the blocks might be taken away. So before you throw, you need to decide which action is worth more to you, and which has the least costs associated with it.

Simple economics.

So why is this golden rule so golden? I think the reason for the glittery goldenness of the golden rule is that it focuses you on tipping the balance of the cost-benefit analysis in your favour. It's quite simple, really. If you make it your problem, they won't really care. If you make it their problem, they will. If the cost to them of being naughty is small, they'll keep being naughty. If the cost to them outweighs any benefits from being naughty, they'll stop.

Of course all this flies in the face of 'modern' thinking about managing children's behaviour, which is all about giving loads and loads of praise and rewards for good behaviour. In this 'child-centred' view, the idea is that we make the rewards for good behaviour so strong they'll automatically choose to be good.

So what could possibly be wrong with that?

Well, in my experience I think it overlooks the fact that

being naughty is ferociously good fun. It just is. Being good is great, and ticks on star charts and pats on the head are all fine and well, but there is something utterly compelling about being naughty. I don't see this as a bad thing — it's just the way we are. If we were all naturally good, we wouldn't need the police and prisons. The bitter truth about us *Homo sapiens* is that being naughty is a powerful reinforcer all by itself.

Being nice to your little sister is great, but pushing her over is also pretty cool when you're three and a control freak. Eating dinner nicely is fine, but throwing the plate across the room when you're bored is also hilariously funny. Similarly, staying in bed at night is perfectly reasonable, but nowhere near as enticing as the thought of running down the hall shrieking at the top of your lungs. You can poop in the toilet if you want the pat on the head, but dropping a big log on the living-room floor is far more entertaining.

The truth is that praise and rewards will only get you so far with children. Ultimately, they will be drawn to the dark side of the Force, they will want the thrill and power that comes from bucking against the system. The only way to stop that stuff in its tracks, at least in my experience, is to make the cost of doing it far outweigh any benefits.

However, there is a key warning sign you need to put the golden rule to work. And it's so simple it's astounding. Basically, if you're dealing with any kind of bad behaviour — be it naughtiness, whining, not staying in bed, sibling conflict or whatever — the rule of thumb is: work out who is feeling the most wound up by it. If it's you, then you need to shift the balance back onto them. If you're feeling more angry/stressed/wound up about it than they are, then the system is out of balance. If you're telling them off and they're acting like they don't care — or, worse, that the whole thing is a big laugh — then you need to shift the balance back onto them.

Ask yourself this question: Whose problem is this right now — theirs or mine? If the answer comes back that it's yours, then it's time to act.

The first thing to understand is that the golden rule (don't make their problem your problem) is a rule you apply whenever you and your little one disagree over what should be happening. So it's not a specific technique, *per se*, but an attitude, an approach. It's about making the consequences for what they do bigger. You increase the cost of the bad behaviour until it becomes so expensive they can't afford it any more.

Here are a few examples to show you what I mean in a very practical way.

➡ If little Timmy laughs when he's in time out and comes out acting as though he doesn't care, simply leave him in time out longer, until the boredom wears out all his cheeky good humour.
➡ If Jane keeps getting out of bed at bedtime and running into the lounge and driving you crazy when you're trying to watch telly, then put her back in her room and lock the door until she gets the point that if you come out of your room, it's going to cost you a bit of isolation.

→ If Mary won't eat her greens, it costs her dessert.
→ If George can't play nicely, it costs him increasing amounts of time sitting by himself.

So the next time you find yourself frustrated, flummoxed, and generally confused about what to do next, just ask yourself this simple question: Whose problem is this? If the answer is that it's yours, then all you need to do is shift the balance so the cost of what they're doing becomes so expensive they simply can't afford to keep doing it. You might be surprised how much this simple focusing thought can shift the commanding heights of the naughty economy in your home.

23
'Go outside and play'

Many modern parents have become quasi cruise-ship entertainment directors. We feel it's our duty to provide our dear ones with constant entertainment and activities. Somehow it became our job to keep boredom at bay. Modern parents spend endless hours painting pictures with toddlers, building Lego towers, and playing dollies.

Now, I'm not saying we shouldn't spend time with our kids, far from it, but I do think things have gone a bit doolally. I don't see why I should have to play all the time. I did that stuff when I was a kid. It was quite fun then; not so much fun now. Now it gets boring very quickly. I've been a kid, I did my time. Now I want to be a grown-up.

My parents just told me to go outside and play when I was a kid. When my dad was watching the cricket on the telly and I complained of boredom, he told me to be quiet and go outside and play. I bet he never worried about bruising my fragile little self-esteem, or whether I would feel that my man-stuff was being neglected. I think all he worried about was whether we'd win the cricket.

And here's the other weird thing: my fragile little self-esteem wasn't bruised, or at least if it was then it healed pretty quickly, because I don't remember feeling bad. I also didn't feel cheated out of doing man-stuff with my dad. I just felt bored, so I went outside and, amazingly, I played.

Just like that.

One Saturday morning, my son came to me just as I had poured a cup of coffee and started reading the newspaper.

'Dadda,' he said, looking up at me with his beautiful, sparkling, little-boy eyes, 'I'm bored.'

'Are you?' I responded, sipping my coffee slowly.

He nodded.

'Well, my beloved first-born son,' I replied, looking down at him with all the concern and love a father has for his boy on a bright and sunny Saturday morning, 'I'm not. I have a cup of coffee and this paper to read. Go outside and play.'

And he did.

What can I say, it's in the genes.

24
Talk is cheap

If you have any doubt of that, just listen to how much your average politician says, and consider how much of it actually means anything. Clearly, if talk had some intrinsic value these people wouldn't throw it around like it can be plucked by the handful from the nearest tree.

Generally, we judge people by their actions, not by their words. Our children are just as smart. To a large extent this is our fault, because we stupidly teach them that while sticks and stones may break their bones, words will never hurt them. This might not have been the cleverest thing to do.

If we had any sense we'd be teaching them that sticks and stones are nothing compared with a harsh word from Mum or Dad. Sticks and stones are like a tickle compared with being told off. Being told off will cause the worst kind of suffering imaginable. Being told off can snap a kid like a twig.

As a result, when a parent goes into the extended parental diatribe (aka nagging), kids pretty much ignore it. You can talk, and talk, and talk, but they pretty much know it's all just words.

You can appeal to their sense of fairness. Yeah, right.

You can ask them to imagine how you feel when they don't listen. Uh huh.

You can argue the logic of your position. Good luck with that one.

All of these approaches will ultimately fail. If you want them to do something, when they won't do what you ask, you have to *do* something to them. You can lecture until you're blue in the face, but they will either nod vacantly, sleep through it with their eyes open, or simply get up and leave.

There is a reason we judge people by their actions, and that is because actions tell you how serious the person is. If you constantly threaten and never follow through, you are the parenting equivalent of the United Nations. No one is going to take you all that seriously. No one is going to put down their weapons. They will simply continue to loot and pillage as you stand about quietly mumbling about various resolutions. If you want to be ignored, then certainly endless talking, nagging, and threatening are good ways to achieve that goal. If you want your kids to listen, then you must act. Stop all the talking and make some examples.

Don't be the UN, be the rebel warlord who demands respect and loyalty in return for protection and access to hijacked aid packages. People might roll their eyes at the UN, but you can bet your bottom dollar that when the rebel warlord walks into the room they'll stand up and politely tip their hat. Don't talk. Shut up and *do*.

25
War of the whiners

One of the many things they never tell you about when you sign up for the whole parenting gig is the particular joy of whiny children. Nothing can prepare you for this.

Taken in isolation the act of whining does not seem especially arduous. A snapshot of a whiny moment can look, to the passing observer, as if it weren't that bad. Usually, said moment involves a parent busy with some task or other as a small child makes noises which sound something like the bleating of a small lamb, or perhaps even the incessant tweeting of a tiny bird.

As a snapshot, these moments seem almost idyllic as the age-old drama plays out where the doting child plays for the attention of the beloved parent.

Yeah, right.

In reality, whining works on very much the same principle as the more subtle forms of torture. It might not be as overtly painful (none of your fingernails is pulled out, after all), but the cumulative effect of the little-lamb-bleating and/or tiny-bird-tweeting is to actually make you want to pull your own fingernails out all by yourself. Anything to escape the constant, never-endingness of it.

You see it isn't the volume, *per se*, that's the problem, or even the content of what they're saying — because sometimes the child whines simply with the use of tone, a piercing whine that seems to have the basic semblance of words, but in fact is just a rolling word-like whine — it's actually the fact that it goes on and on and on and on. And on and on. And on and on and on and on and on and on and on.

Whining, quite simply, sucks the will to live.

Whining also teaches us who we *really* are. Remember how before you had kids and you thought you were going to be the calm parent, the soothing, loving, understanding, patient, attentive and Zen-like parent? And remember how your first experience of sustained whining blew all that nonsense away? Most of us have been there ... that feeling where your ability to restrain the urge to scream is reduced to a desperate fingernails-on-the-edge-of-the-ledge clawing grasp. Sometimes we manage to hang on, and sometimes the sheer weight of the whining pulls us from the ledge and it all ends in bellowing, tears, and the inevitable guilts.

That little people all seem to spontaneously develop the ability to whine is a sure sign that it has to be a useful technique. They don't go to classes to learn this stuff, or read about it on some blog and then decide to give it a go: the ability to whine seems to arise both spontaneously and independently. In much the same way as little baby hippos learn to wallow, the little person learns to whine.

Why is this? To answer that question we need to recall the basic goal of each and every little person: they want to rule the world. This is not such an outrageous goal when you realize they're starting from the basic premise that everything in the world is theirs. If they can see it, it's theirs. If someone else has it, it's still theirs. If you won't give it to them, this is desperately unfair because it was actually theirs to begin with.

The only problem they have is a height restriction. If they had another metre or so, then they would have no need for us because they could just march on in and do whatever they wanted and get whatever they wanted. In lieu of this extra height, they quickly learn that whining is a simple way to get what they want. As a baby they learn that if they whine (or cry, which is the less sophisticated but incredibly effective baby version of whining), then they can get fed, changed, cuddled, swaddled, walked, cootchy-cooed at, or any one of a number of different and interesting outcomes. Essentially we teach them to whine because we reinforce the behaviour.

And it's been going on since we lived in caves. Crying gets them what they want as babies, and over time they experiment with different pitches, volumes, and variations until they perfect the exact type of whining which causes their parents the maximum psychological distress and pain. Then they do it over and over until you give them what they want.

When you think about the basic rationale for whining, the ways to make it worse are as painfully obvious as the whining itself. If you reward the whining, if you give in to it, it will get worse. If you reward the slight niggly whining, before you know it you will be barricaded inside your bathroom, head in hands, feeling like a total failure and on the verge of complete mental breakdown.

Whatever you do, do not reward whining. It might buy you some short-term peace, but the long-term cost is huge. Whatever you reward will come back for more, and the next time the whining will be that much more intense because you've shown them that if they just push hard enough you'll eventually crack and give them what they want. That way lies madness.

Just as the underlying driving forces of whining are pretty basic, the way you deal to it is equally simple. Just as the little person thinks that everything is theirs, and that they rule all they can see, it's our job to teach them that this isn't the case. It's our job to teach them how to rein in their megalomania and learn the subtle social rules needed to get along in the world. We have to teach them that whining is an ineffective strategy for getting what they want: no one likes whining, which means they'll end up with less, not more. Here are five tips for doing that.

→ **Distraction** This is one of the simplest and easiest tricks to use. If you're being whined at, then distraction is the most benign of all the approaches. Instead of raising your voice, look up in a dramatic fashion, cock your head to one side, and say (in a dramatic voice): 'Do you hear that? Eagles.' The little person will more likely than not look up as well and listen closely to see if they can hear said eagles. It doesn't have to be eagles — it can just as easily be monkeys, fairies, lions, ponies, or flying fish. Anything will do. Just distract them on to some other thing (real or actual) and there's a good chance you'll get a little reprieve from the whinies.

➡ **Ignore the whining**   This one is a bit harder, because ignoring whining is like trying to ignore someone scraping their fingernails down a blackboard which, for reasons that are hard to understand, is inside your head. But if you can ignore the whining, they'll get the message that there's no payoff in the behaviour. That said, I've found that simply ignoring the whining isn't usually enough, so you'll need to team this one up with the next one on the list.

➡ **Reward non-whining behaviour**   It's an oldie, but a goodie. You're trying to teach them that the way to get what they want is to be a little more considerate and not to whine, so make a real effort to notice and reward the non-whiny stuff. This can be anything. It can even be standing quietly for a few seconds. Whatever you do, you need to make sure that they get the idea that whining gets you nothing and not whining tends to end more happily.

➡ **Walk it off**   The power of exercise to clear the air is quite miraculous. It doesn't have to be a 10-day hike into the Himalayas; just a stroll down to the mailbox will sometimes do. Just get a bit of activity going on and a change of scene. Often this is just as important for your state of mind as theirs.

➡ **Time out**   If all else fails, fall back on the basics. Ask them to stop nicely, tell them what will happen if they keep whining, then if they're still going you put them in time out. This gives them the very simple message that whiners tend to end up with nothing. Simple, but important.

We all have to put up with whining; there's no way around that one, sadly. That said, if you keep in mind what drives the behaviour, you're likely to avoid the biggest trap of all which is to reward the whining. Teach them instead that people who ask for things nicely, and who know how to accept no for an answer, tend to live happier, more contented lives. Thus your home will be a much easier place to be.

26
'I *hate* you'

No they don't. Not by a long shot. Hatred is something that takes years of hard work to develop, and most of us probably wouldn't be able to spare that much time. It's far too hard to get your kids to hate you, so my advice is: don't try. Get them to love you. It's easier. As I said earlier, all you have to do is feed 'em and give 'em somewhere to sleep, and just about that alone will get you at least some kind of half-arsed love.

Hatred takes serious effort. The 'I hate you' statement is a perfect example of little people learning how to mess with big people's heads. The problem occurs when the big people stop thinking and take it seriously. If you take it seriously it will likely rip out your heart, so why would you? Still, surprisingly many parents do, and not surprisingly it messes them up. This is the little person's intention from the beginning, because in the ensuing tears, dust, and confusion, the little people overrun your position and immediately set about establishing new forward command posts (see *All they want is to rule the world*).

The 'I hate you' technique is the childhood equivalent of the 'flash-bang' explosive device that SWAT and anti-terrorist teams use when trying to breach barricaded buildings: all noise and blinding lights designed to frighten and confuse. The primary goal of the use of a flash-bang device in situations of armed conflict is to confuse and incapacitate. Sound familiar? They will say they hate you, but really it's just a ploy. They simply want to knock you off-balance, and then rule the world.

The trick is having a good comeback. Ignore it. Sing in a loud operatic style about the tragedy of the mother hated by her daughter. Grasp your chest, grunt painfully, and fall to the ground. Look at them with joyously tearful eyes, and tell them in a completely over-the-top voice how you love them because they say the *swee-ee-ee-eetest* things. Chase them, grab them in a bear hug, and squeeze the bad stuff out (best squeeze until you feel their bones creak, though). Reply with an angry KGB officer diatribe in Russian (if you can't speak Russian, then simply repeat 'Burrshky Molotov' over and over). Any of these techniques, or a hundred other silly ones, will do.

They don't hate you, so don't take it seriously. If you do, then you're a mug.

27
Loving is easy, liking is hard

The only parents who like their children *all* the time are the people in commercials for nappies. They seem to be just so gosh-diddly-darned happy about just about every gosh-diddly-darned thing. For them bowel motions aren't a chore, they're a joy. Conversations in their house would probably go something like this:

'Oh, look: Tarquin just did a little poop-diddly-oopy. Fantastic.'

'My turn.'

'Oh, that's not fair — you got to change him last time.'

'I know, but I just love-diddly-wove him so much.'

'Well … alright, but that means I get to clean up the next two pukes.'

'Deal-diddly-eel.'

The rest of us are not quite so consistently full of the joys of children. The rest of us take very little pleasure in the miracle of bowel motions. Children are a joy, and a miracle, and a blessing, and all that yah-de-yah-de-yah — just not all the time. Actually, for those of us who've been in it for a while, you soon come to learn that along with all the miracles, and the blessings, and the yah-de-yah-de-yah, there are some quite significant stretches which are tedious, frustrating, and occasionally completely gross.

As a brief example, when my son was eight weeks old he vomited on my wife one night as she was feeding him. This was not an ordinary vomit, though, because no ordinary vomit could encompass the dimensions of that night. I was watching telly, heard a noise that sounded like a small, rather liquid burp, and turned around to see that my wife had been partially submerged in a sea of pale violet slime. The pool was so deep and vast it rippled when she moved. It was clear to me that a doorway to another, much grosser dimension had briefly opened, and disgorged on her a universe of sick.

She looked at me imploringly, much as one might if one were slowly sinking into a great pool of bile, and to my great shame I have to confess that my first thought was simply to run. To run until I could run no more, and start my life again in some warmer, cleaner place.

I didn't run.

But it was close.

This, of course, is the great trick that our genes play on us to get us to make more of them. Before we have children, our genes fill our heads with nappy commercials so that we fall into the grand adventure of raising children with completely unrealistic expectations. Our genes also cunningly make newborn babies fairly innocuous little souls for the first 10 to 14 days to give us a chance to bond with them. They gurgle and coo their way into our lives, and by the time they finally fully wake up it's too late. We are bonded and there is no going back.

We sometimes let the delicious fantasies play out in our

heads of leaving them on the church steps, but when push comes to shove we invariably chicken out. We always go back and get them again after only a block or so.

Have to live with 'em, can't live without 'em.

So the loving is compulsory, our genes take care of that one, but the liking is completely voluntary. I have two boys, and they are my heart. This is decidedly inconvenient, because it means that my life is not my own any more. Actually my life is unimportant, because they are my life. I don't mean that in some kind of over-the-top, living-my-life-through-them, hovering-over-every-aspect-of-what-they-do kind of way, but emotionally they are my life. I would walk into the fire for them, literally, because that's what a dad does. If there were only two seats in the lifeboat, I would put one on one seat, and the other on my knee. If there was only one seat, then I'd be screwed.

None of this, however, means that I *like* them all the time.

Actually, there are many, many moments when I don't like them. This is only fair, because there are many moments when they don't like me. Just the other night my son passed a note out under his bedroom door (which had been handily converted into a prison cell by virtue of a small bolt from the local hardware store), and on the note he had written his mother's name with little hearts around it, his brother's name with little hearts around it, and my name which had been crossed out in multiple black scribbles. I took this as a positive sign that I was doing my job, because if your kids like you all the time then you're probably being a bit soft.

What is important, though, is that we like each other *most* of the time, or at least the majority of the time. Liking is the fun part, it's the goofing-around part, the part where we get to be silly, and crack stupid jokes. Liking is fun, and fun is the grease of family life. Without some liking, without some fun, the whole thing will eventually grind to a halt.

A mum once said to me, 'We don't do silly in our house.' That troubled me greatly, because in my experience the families who end up in the greatest distress are the ones where there is no fun. Fun is the stuff that keeps the wheels moving.

But you cannot like them all the time. You just can't. Maybe the parents on a nappy commercial can, but that's only 15 seconds. We don't get to see what happens when the camera turns off. My guess is their kids end up seeing shrinks, talking about how their parents just never stopped gosh-diddly-darned smiling all the damn time. That's just not right.

So don't feel you have to like your kids all the time, because you don't, you can't. But you do need to like them for the majority of the time, and they need to feel liked for the majority of the time. As with everything it's about common sense and moderation.

Liked all the time: impossible.

Liked most of the time: good.

Liked none of the time: very, very bad.

Life is not a nappy commercial — and we all need to be thankful for that small mercy.

28
Credible threats

Following on from the whole warlord thing (see earlier chapter *Talk is cheap*) is the doctrine of credible threats. This is very simple, and essentially holds that you should never make empty threats. Threats are all about leverage, and you only get leverage when the crowbar is real. Imaginary crowbars can't shift rocks. If you use an imaginary crowbar, you just end up looking like some kind of crazy person waving their arms at the rock.

Don't threaten to do something unless you mean to do it.

For example, if you say to your fighting children 'If you guys don't cut it out then I swear I'm going to give you both away', you actually have to give at least one of them away or they will completely ignore you. That might seem a little harsh, but imagine the look of shock and surprise on their face when their new family turns up to claim them. Imagine the tears of remorse and promises to be better as you pack their little bags and bundle them off in the back of the truck with the mean-looking people who run the local chimney-sweeping business.

Now, imagine how seriously the rest of your remaining children will take you the next time you threaten to give them away if they don't stop fighting. You can bet they're going to listen pretty quickly.

So please, please, please, be a responsible parent. Don't threaten them with stuff that you aren't going to do. If you threaten to give them away, then away they must be given.

It isn't cruel, not really.

Being given away is how children learn.

29
Walk the talk

This is one of those perennial parenting gems that gets passed out all the time with the ginger nuts and the cups of tea. It's a good solid theory, it makes sense, it's true, and like most things to do with raising children in the real world, most of us struggle to attain the gold standard for this one. Very few people have sufficient moral fibre to practise what they preach; the rest of us just have to fudge our way through those uncomfortable moments when our fundamental human inconsistencies shine through.

'Dadda?'

'Yes, son.'

'You know how you said that we have to listen to the police and that it's wrong to break the law?'

'Yes, son.'

'So why are you going over the speed limit now?'

'What?'

'Why are you going 60 when it should be 50?'

'Uuhhh ... well, even though the limit is 50 the police don't mind too much if you go a little bit over that.'

'But isn't it still breaking the law?'

'Well, technically yes, but it's not like *really, really* breaking the law.'

'So it's alright to break the law a little bit?'

'No ... well, I mean ... it's complicated, son. Big-people stuff. Hey, you wanna get an ice cream?'

Tricky stuff, this practising what you preach. The problem is we try to set our kids up with the concrete ideals, and then hope that as they grow older they'll learn to accommodate a greyer shade of things. Yes, it's wrong to break the law, but almost all of us do on a fairly regular basis.

Perhaps one of the most common and most glaring examples of not practising what we preach as a parent is when we yell at our kids for yelling. Logically doesn't make much sense, does it? I yell at you to try to get across my point that yelling is not acceptable behaviour. If I'm being completely honest, the thing I personally yell at my own dear sweet boys the most is 'STOP YELLING!' I'd love to be able to say I always take them aside and have a reasoned discussion about the issues, but more often than not I bellow.

So let's not pretend for a moment that we're all going to practise what we preach all the time, because it's an impossible standard for most of us. But this 'practise what you preach' issue is one of the things modern parents agonize over and wallow about in, because we worry that our obvious hypocrisy and lack of consistency will somehow damage our kids' young and fragile psyches. If you're totally inconsistent and chaotic, and you work really hard at making your kids miserable and confused, then you probably will. For the vast majority of us, however, a little dose of double standards usually doesn't result in any long-term harm. If it did, we'd all be in trouble because our parents were just as human as us.

Having said that, abandoning any attempt at modelling decent behaviour is both lazy and inherently bad for your kids. They look to us to see how they should behave. You can't say mean things to other people all the time and then expect your kids to speak nicely to you. You also can't bad-mouth their teachers in front of them and then expect them to behave in school (although I'm constantly amazed at how many parents don't seem able to grasp this fundamental fact). We are their most important reference material when it comes to designing their own policies for navigating through the world.

They watch us, and they copy what we do, both the good and the bad.

So how do you be a real person and a role model at the same time?

As with most things in life, the answer lies somewhere in the middle ground. We have to set the tone for how to behave, and how to treat other people, yet also teach them that not everything in life is always 100% consistent. If you can't learn to deal with a little hypocrisy, you're going to spend much of your life outraged, writing letters to the editor, and hanging around with other crazy, outraged people.

These are my suggestions for how to find that bumpy middle ground:

→ **Stay on message** Figure out what you're preaching about, and try to work as hard as you can to stay on that message. If you're preaching about talking nicely to people, try as hard as you can to talk nicely to people. A bit obvious I know, but sometimes we miss the simplest most obvious steps.

- **Acknowledge your slip-ups**   If you do something wrong, or that goes against your sermon, then say it. Don't do this for every last little thing, because that gets boring pretty quickly, but you should say when you've crossed an important line.
- **Tell them that everyone makes mistakes**   Even parents make mistakes. The important thing isn't that you screwed up, it's what you learn from it and what you do about it. This helps kids begin to understand that the world isn't really very black and white, and that coping with greys, and inconsistencies, and unfairness is part of the deal.
- **Teach them that none of us is perfect**   What really matters is striving to make things better, rather than doing the same crappy thing over and over.

It's also my firm view — and part of my own parenting practice — to point out to the little person that the reason daddas are sometimes allowed to yell when kids aren't is because I'm a grown-up and so the rules are different. If they don't agree with that, I usually point out, they're more than welcome to get a job, buy their own house, and make up their own rules.

If it's close by, I might even come visit.

30
Fighting

Children fight. This is as natural as the sun rising. It would be nice to think that they would embrace the philosophy of pacifism and conflict resolution, but of course they won't. Gandhi may have got the British out of India through non-violent non-cooperation, but I bet even the Mahatma was mean to his little sisters once or twice while growing up.

You have a couple of choices on this front. The first is that you can don your sandals and raise your children in a totally non-violent home. You can take them aside whenever they hit each other and patiently explain why violence is wrong. You can also redirect and distract and praise them like billy-oh for walking away rather than clobbering their siblings.

The other option — and I must say it is the one we utilize in our house — is simply to tell them to go fight outside. This option works very well. There are some provisos, however. You must impose some limits: rules such as no kicking, and no punching in the head or below their wee belt (potentially too harmful), also no pinching, scratching, or biting (too girly). Shoving is fine. Punches to the arm are fine. Wrestling and pinning, all good.

I've heard the argument that we live in such a violent world we have a duty to teach children not to be violent. I agree. There is, however, a difference between violence and beating the living crap out of your brother. The first is wrong; the second is the absolute right of every child. I see no moral ambiguity or double standard here, although I'm sure I'll get emails from angry hippies who think there is.

My theory is this, though: if you're going to annoy anyone, best annoy the hippies because at least you know they'll never come up and clobber you. If you're going to be mean to anyone, be mean to hippies.

There is also the tactical issue of size differences. Older siblings have the physical edge on their younger, smaller counterparts which can be a real difficulty if you run a 'go outside and fight' economy. We addressed this issue in our house by going to our local toy store and buying my younger son a plastic sword. In this way my older son learned never to pick on little guys with swords, and my younger son for his part learned that one should always pack some heat.

See, all's well that ends well.

31
What the CIA and KGB could learn from bedtime chats

Bedtime chats are a powerful tool. There is little that can compare with a bedtime chat in terms of intelligence gathering. The KGB and CIA should read this to find out a thing or two about finding out a thing or two. You don't need thumb-screws or sodium pentothal, no need to take people off to military prisons in Cuba or the gulags of the proverbial Soviet archipelagos: all you need is a bedtime chat.

Instead of all that running around ducking and diving during the Cold War, Khrushchev should have just popped around to the White House at bedtime and sat on the end of Kennedy's bed and had a bit of a chin-wag. In 10 minutes or so he would have found out everything he needed to know.

Now, you may not be interested in finding out about the advances your children are making with their nuclear development programmes, or their plans for world domination, but you might want to know how they're doing generally. You might also want them to know that you *want* to know how they're doing generally. It's good for your kids to feel that you're interested in them and their lives, because if they don't think that you're all in trouble.

The nice thing about bedtime chats is that all the usual stuff that parents and kids fight over has been done by then. Dinner has been eaten, teeth have been brushed, and they've had their final niggle at their older/younger siblings. By bedtime, pretty much the only thing left to do is chat. It doesn't have to be a great big deal. We're not talking world summit here, we're just talking about a chat.

It's also a good time to debrief anything that happened during the day that might have been not so great. For example, if your dear one lost their wee rag you can chat about what happened that made them feel like that, and what they think they could do differently next time. Bedtime chats are great for helping your kids gain wisdom from hindsight. It's also a good time to teach them how to problem-solve. Quite aside from all that, it can be kind of cool to hang out for a while, unpressured by routines or timetables, and just chat. Imagine that: just chatting?

So next time you find yourself wondering what the hell is going on with your kid, don't reach for the thumbscrews, try something different. Wait until bedtime and have a chat with them instead. Hang out for a few minutes and see where it leads. I guarantee they'll be some of the best conversations of your life. When you're old and sitting in the retirement home you won't remember talking to your boss about the new computer system, but you will remember sitting on your kid's bed discussing whether elephant poo and dinosaur poo would smell the same.

32
School in less than 450 words

School is fantastic. Not only do they take your kids from 9 a.m. to 3.00 p.m. five days a week, but they also teach them stuff. All that and learning, too! The secret with school is not to get all anal about it. Don't get all carried away.

The first day of school will probably be the worst for you. For most of us it's the first time we leave our wee one at the mercy of the pack. In pre-school or kindergarten there is always an adult who has them in line of sight. At school they are thrust out into the big mean world without anyone there to save them. The first day of school will involve at least some level of fretting on your part.

And from this point on, the amount of control and influence you have over their lives will slowly fade.

It has become very fashionable of late to gradually introduce children to school over a number of weeks and a number of visits. Don't fret too much about this. Do it if you can, don't if you can't. In the end, the variables which influence how your child experiences school are mostly out of your control anyway, so don't get your knickers all twisted up over that one.

And when they are in there and settled, don't get all anxious and silly about the whole education thing. A principal once told me that he'd been approached by the mother of a six-year-old who wanted a copy of the syllabus for the next term so they could get a 'jump-start' on learning. Jump-start? You jump-start cars; I don't think you jump-start six-year-olds. The only jumping a six-year-old should be doing is onto something, off something, or over something.

Relax. Get to know your kids' teachers, but not in a pushy, hang-around-and-talk-for-ages-after-class kind of way. After class they just want to get their work done and go home. Fair enough. Who wouldn't? Be involved in your school community by all means, just don't be a pain. If there are bumps along the way it is far better if you actually know your kids' teachers. Better still if they don't think you're a pain.

If your kids come out of school having made a few friends and most of all having learned that learning is fun, then you can tick that box. The world is changing so fast that it's silly to think you can ever stop learning. You will never know enough. In the new world the most important commodity will be the ability to constantly learn.

Oh, and so far as home-schooling goes: What are you? Insane?

33
Give teachers a break ... don't whine!

Teachers have to put up with an enormous amount of crap from anxious, often well-meaning but utterly annoying parents. Teachers work very hard, they do a lot they never get paid for, and by and large are a fantastic group of people. I've worked in schools for years and am often in awe of the dedication and commitment teachers show towards their pupils. There are bad eggs, to be sure, but as a general rule teachers are great.

What is unfortunate is that they have to put up with more than their fair share of whining. Again, I'm not saying don't be involved with your school, and I'm not saying don't question things, or even that you shouldn't advocate for your kids if it's warranted, but I *am* saying don't whine.

If you do whine, they will simply smile politely at you, listen patiently, and then talk about you in the staffroom. The reason they will do this is because they are not allowed to slap you. They are, however, allowed to *imagine* slapping you.

Before you go in and whine at the teachers, make sure you have your facts straight. It could well be true, for instance, that the bigger boy who clobbered your boy is a bully, but it could also be that your boy was being very annoying. Not all clobbering in schools is about bullying; sometimes it's simply how the bigger kids teach the little kids not to be a pain in the arse.

You also don't want to be rescuing your kids all the time. If there's a fire, then sure, rescue away, I have no issue with that at all, but don't rescue them from strife at school. Life and strife rhyme for a very good reason: they go together. You can't have one without the other, so you need to learn to deal with it. Let them fight their own battles; you've probably got enough of your own to be getting on with.

So be involved, by all means, just don't be a pain in the arse.

34
How to solve the problem of homework forever

Many parents struggle with the homework issue. It causes more conflict than just about any other thing. Tarquin and Portia come home tired and grumpy, or maybe they just get busy doing something that's more fun. Mum is usually the first person to ask the question that starts previously happy homes spiralling down into noisy, unhappy mayhem: 'Have you done your homework?' And then it all begins.

Parents all over the world struggle with how to get kids to do homework. Whole books have been written about it. Most parenting books devote at least a chapter to it. They suggest things like establishing routines, giving kids a nice work space, rewards, consequences — all the usual palaver. Most of which, of course, don't work. The reason for this is very simple: homework sucks. It always has, and it always will. It doesn't matter what you do to make it less suckful, it will always suck. This is one of the fundamental truths of the universe.

Homework fights can destroy family life. They turn what might have been a nice evening into a nightmare for some parents. You push, and cajole, and bribe, and do everything you can to establish good homework habits, and when you do luck out and find something that works you can be sure it has a pretty short shelf-life.

OK, Mr Smarty-pants, I hear you ask, so what's your wonderful idea? How can you fix the homework problem forever?

Simple. Don't do it.

Most readers will probably be thinking this is an idiotic suggestion. Are you crazy? How will they all become doctors, lawyers, and accountants if they don't have homework? Well, let me tell you a little secret about schools and why they give homework. Many of them don't believe that homework serves any useful purpose, and research on the effectiveness of homework is anything but conclusive. The only thing we can really deduce with any certainty is that the evidence is completely inconclusive. At best there is a weak positive effect for high-school-aged kids, but the younger you go the more the evidence disappears. The case for giving homework to primary-/elementary-aged kids is about as strong as the evidence for weapons of mass destruction in Iraq. People might tell you that it's true, but when you look you just can't find any.

So why do teachers give homework, you ask?

This is a very good question, and one I posed to a number of principals at a primary school principals' conference I was speaking at. They *all* said the same thing: they do it simply because if they didn't they would have an avalanche of anxious parents banging on their office door demanding that poor little Tarquin not be deprived of his God-given right to an education. There were a couple of principals who had actually tried to get rid of homework and this is exactly what had happened. The parents hated it. In my experience, what teachers say publicly about homework, and what they say privately, is not always the same thing.

The other criticism is that, without the structure of regular homework, lazy disinterested parents will not take any kind of interest in their kids' education. Should we think that through a little? What on earth makes anyone think that these people are taking any kind of useful interest via homework in the first place? If you don't give a rat's arse about what your kids are doing in school, the presence of homework in a schoolbag probably isn't going to make any difference one way or the other. These kids are pretty much doing it solo regardless of what's in their bag.

I've also heard that homework is a great 'bonding experience' between children and parents. Do I even need to comment on that one? I think not. Some statements are just so inherently stupid they are their own rebuttal.

My advice would be to do the homework if your kids enjoy it and it isn't a fight. If there is too much resistance then don't push it, just don't do it. The last thing you want your kids to learn is that learning is a chore. Cleaning up your room is a chore; learning should be fun. The last thing we need to be teaching the PlayStation generation is that reading is a chore. There are all kinds of ways to teach kids that learning is fun; homework is usually about the worst of them. Here are five suggestions to get you started:

- ➡ Find a book on something they actually like and read that.
- ➡ Surf the web for interesting/fun sites, and read them.
- ➡ Write letters to grandparents and cousins.
- ➡ Go to the zoo and read displays there.
- ➡ Read the back-cover blurb of their favourite DVDs.

That's just for starters, and that's just reading. There's all manner of fun stuff you can do that doesn't have to take a long time and doesn't have to be boring.

So, if you want to stop homework fights forever, don't do it.

Simple, huh?

35
Self-control

When you think about it, self-control is one of the most basic skills that we need to get through life. Self-control is what gets you through when your idiot boss tells you he needs that report by five o'clock when he's known about it for three days. Self-control is what gets you through when you're trying to lose a bit of weight and you see the best white chocolate muffins in the history of muffins sitting on the counter right in front of you as you go to pay for your trim flat white. Self-control is also what gets you through when your precious little one breaks the window with the ball that you've told them not to kick inside a thousand times.

Self-control is a very good thing.

Up until very recently, though, we didn't know just how good it was. Then in 2010 the group of researchers we met in the earlier chapter *Bolshy toddlers* published a paper on the impact of self-control on children's lives. It is one of the most amazing scientific papers I have ever read (and trust me, I've read a few), and it also has really important implications for anyone in the business of making and growing little people.

What is self-control? Well, it's about delaying gratification (waiting rather than grabbing what's in front of your face), controlling impulses (not dumping your popcorn over Mr Big Head who is blocking your view at the movies), and reining in your emotions (not screaming at your partner who went all the way to the supermarket and brought back everything except the can of pineapple pieces you specifically asked for). It's also a fundamental part of self-discipline, conscientiousness, and perseverance. Particular parts of the brain are involved in exercising self-control, and genetic and environmental influences also affect how good we are at it.

Now, before we get into the nitty-gritty, promise me you'll read the whole thing, because there's good news following the not-so-good — so panic not!

OK, here goes. Essentially, the researchers found that while self-control is a good omen, kids with low self-control tend to have all kinds of problems later in life. If you had low self-control as a child, you were more likely to have problems with alcohol and drugs, become a teen parent, have financial problems, and have problems with your career. You also were more likely to experience health problems later in life.

Now don't break out in a cold sweat if you think your little person has very little self-control and therefore is now doomed to a life of substance abuse, teen pregnancy, and crime. Because along with the bad news there's plenty of good news as well. Research shows that self-control can be developed over the lifespan, and those children who do have to learn it end up doing better as a result.

This is important, so I'll just say it again: even if you have low self-control as a child, you can learn to develop self-control as you grow, and this will have real benefits in your life. So the big message for all us parents is not that poor self-control is bad, but that we can help our little one to develop self-control, and the more we do that the better they will be.

So how do we do that? Here's the really cool bit, because the way that you teach children to develop this amazing, life-changing skill is just by doing all those good old-fashioned things that good mums and dads have been doing ever since children were invented. You don't have to buy any special equipment or learn a special technique or special magical words. You just keep doing what you've always been doing.

Think about what self-control involves — delaying grati-fication, managing your feelings, controlling your impulses, persevering, and being conscientious — and it all becomes much simpler. All you need to do is help them to see the con-nection between those things and the payoffs, and then give them plenty of chances to practise self-control. Here are a few ideas to get you started ... most of which you will almost certainly already be doing:

➡ Reward good behaviour and punish bad behaviour. Motivate them to control those little impulses and focus on the longer-term reward.
➡ Don't give them everything they want whenever they want it. Make them wait for things from time to time. Waiting is a skill that needs practice.
➡ Teach them that sometimes you have to do things you don't like (eg, picking up your toys) to get access to things you do like (eg, walks in the park).

→ Praise sharing with their friends and others. This helps them to understand that grabbing stuff first isn't as big a payoff as good times with the people you cooperate with.

→ Encourage them not to give up. If they start walking up a hill, don't let them give up just because their little legs get a bit tired. Push on and then make a big deal of the sense of achievement they'll get from doing things that are hard. The best views tend to be from the top of the hill in life, not the bottom.

→ Pay them a pittance when they are old enough for pocket money. They'll learn more if they have to save hard for something, and it will mean more to them when they eventually get it.

→ Model all of these things as much as you can. (See the chapter *Walk the talk*.)

→ Praise effort rather than telling them how clever they are. Instead of saying how clever they are for drawing a dinosaur-ish looking squiggle, tell them what hard workers they are and that the reason they're so good at drawing is because they practise really hard.

→ Teach them that guests choose their biscuits first.

→ Teach them that even if they're angry with you, they still have to speak nicely to you. They'll need this skill when they get their first job working for an idiot. Sometimes you just have to shut up and smile politely.

→ Basically anything and everything that involves them reining in their impulses and focusing on the bigger picture.

It's very important to remember that self-control is not something little people possess in any great amount. Most have very little self-control. If their little line of Matchbox cars is cruelly knocked slightly out of their carefully arranged alignment, many of them will dissolve into tears and tantrums in abundance. If they can't have the dolly with the pink dress, they scream. If you don't give them the blue cup right now the world ends. All this is very normal. It'll probably take them about a decade to master self-control in any meaningful way. Some of us struggle with self-control many decades down the track.

Being impulsive, selfish, instant-reward-oriented, impatient and short-sighted is normal for our young folk. These traits are part of the journey from no control to having as much of it as you can manage. Self-control is important, but just like any life-skill (eg, juggling, lion-taming, solving Rubik's cube) it takes time and a lot of practice.

What's really important is that there's now some very solid science which totally supports all that old common-sense stuff mums and dads have been doing forever. What's especially nice is we can now say with absolute certainty to our children that it really is important to let the guests choose their biscuit first, to share your toys, and to figure out some other thing to do when your little brother annoys you other than clouting him. We can say and know with absolute certainty that we're helping them to be better, healthier, more productive, and happier grown-ups.

And that's the best science of all.

36
They all have to find their own way

Bears have a sensible approach to parenting. When baby bears are about a year or so old, the momma bear chases them up a tree and does a runner. Good for them. Bears clearly understand the importance of independence.

That and speed.

I think one of the key tasks all parents must understand is that, when all the little beans have been counted, the only people who know what's best for our kids are our kids. They're the ones who have to actually live their lives, not us. We can offer guidance, and advice, but they have to bear the brunt of the decisions they make.

I have all kinds of dreams for my boys. I want my older son to join the police and fly helicopters for a while before joining the armed offenders squad and then finally finishing up as a detective on serious inquiries. He will then go on to work at Interpol catching international war criminals. Leisure-wise, I'd like him to do surf life-saving as a teenager and then white-water kayaking as an adult. My younger son will emigrate to the United States and fly F-111 fighter-bombers off the USS *Nimitz*. We will visit him for holidays and he will take me for stomach-churning flights. His call sign will be 'Barnstormer' on account of his frighteningly obsessive passion for supersonic low-level bombing runs. He won't have time for leisure activities because he'll be too busy studying. That's tough, but them's the breaks.

Now, while these are my dreams, I'm pretty sure my boys don't share them. At the moment my older son wants to be a palaeontologist and my younger son wants to be Spiderman. Fair enough.

There's nothing wrong with my dreams for my boys, but there's a lot wrong with me trying to get them to take them on. They'll have plenty of their own. So I hope for Interpol and F-111s, but I'm kind of curious to see what they come up with. They will find their own way, and my job is simply to believe in them.

So we should be more like the bears. We should have faith that they'll be OK, and leave them to get on with it.

Now, am I saying that you should literally chase your kids up a tree and run off?

No, of course not.

Use the car, it's quicker so there's less chance of them catching you.

37
Humourless bastards

A while ago I was doing a guest slot on a radio show. I was, not surprisingly, doing the parenting piece. It was fun and we talked about a bunch of stuff to do with kids. In many ways it was this book, just not written down. There was a bit of email feedback that would come in from time to time, but the email that stands out for me was from a person who took extreme umbrage at my use of the term 'kid'. This person pointed out, with a degree of moral indignation which suggested they may have been wearing underpants one size too small, that 'they're *children*, not *kids*. *Kids* are baby goats.'

Oh dear God, what has the world come to?

From that point on, I made an effort to use the word 'kids' in every second sentence. My aim was simple: I thought if that humourless bastard sitting at home listening got angry enough they might pop a blood vessel. In short, I was trying to kill them using the power of stupid self-righteous indignation. My theory was this: the world has enough stupid people in it already, one less would be good for us all.

It seems to me that we're all worried about the wrong stuff. We worry about climate change, global pandemics, and international terrorism. I think we should be worried about the humourless bastards, because they're the ones who make us all miserable. It's the humourless bastards who ban lolly scrambles in case someone loses an eye. They suck the sunshine out of a summer day. These people sit around, and, when they run out of things to feel offended about themselves, they generously assume offence on someone else's behalf. These people are a menace, because if they had their way we'd all be wearing comfortable slacks and quietly sipping sugarless tea.

It is our sacred duty as parents to do all that we can to prevent our children from growing up into humourless bastards. That is no way to live. Teach them to have a laugh, especially over stuff that we really shouldn't laugh at. Life is far too serious to take seriously. If *you* are a humourless bastard, then please, do the right thing: put your kids up for adoption.

Trust me, they'll have more fun with someone else.

38
Look after the little guy

If there is one message that I hope my boys get, it's that their job is to look after the little guy. That's a message we reinforce a lot at home. I want my boys to be the ones who step up when the little guy is being picked on. I want them to be the ones who include the kid with no friends. I want them to do the right thing when everyone else is doing the opposite.

In some ways this is a dangerous road. Going against the mob is not without its risks, but I think if this troubled world of ours is to have any hope then we should all be trying to stand up for the little guy. Besides, as soon as they're old enough I'm going to make them both do a jujitsu course, so that if negotiation fails they can always pin the bully and twist his arm until he cries like a girl.

When I was nine years old there was a boy in my class whom I'll call John. He had the most freckles of any kid I've ever seen, and so of course this made him an obvious target for the mob. Kids can be cruel, and they were pretty damn cruel to him. John also had trouble with reading and so I was made his 'reading buddy'. I don't remember much about him other than the fact that he was a nice kid, kind of sad and a bit trodden-down, but a nice kid.

One day he'd been given a real roasting at playtime — a bunch of kids kept chanting 'fly-shit face, fly-shit face' — and it all got too much. He ran out of the school grounds in tears. I don't remember much from when I was that age, but I do remember me and a mate running after him and convincing him to come back. We told him to ignore them because they were idiots and that we'd hang out with him. He was crying, but he came back.

Now, I don't remember what happened when we got back to school, and I don't know what happened to John, but I do remember that one moment. Even now it makes me feel proud. I'd like to say I was always that stand-up guy, but of course I wasn't. There were plenty of times when I was a kid when I stood back and let stuff happen, but not that time. That time I was the stand-up guy.

I want my boys to be that guy.

I want them to look back on their childhood knowing that they always stood up for the little guy. How cool would that be?

Also, girls love that stuff.

39
The essentials of goofing off

If you were to ask me what is the single biggest issue facing parents today, I'd reply in a very firm voice that it's taking the whole thing way too seriously. We over-think this parenting stuff far more than is helpful, and in the process we've lost a lot of the fun stuff along the way. Just the other day, for instance, I was reading an online post from a mum who felt guilty because when she took her kids out she did it with her friends, and she was worried that this was somehow letting down the side. That she was cheating her children of quality time because she was chatting and having coffee with her mates.

It is in this rich and fertile ground of parental anxiety that seriousness sprouts like some kind of noxious weed. Seriousness both adds to your stress and sucks the fun out of life. It's like some little beige vampire draining all the good stuff from your day.

If you really want to get serious about something, then get serious about goofing off. Why? Because it's fun, and because it helps you to get through the day. Let's face it, sometimes the day-to-day business of raising children is a bit of a grind. In fact, most days are a bit like that. There's only so much passion and excitement you can generate for shovelling in spoonfuls of mashed carrot. Sure it's quality time, and it's a miracle watching them grow, and all that stuff … but it's still shovelling in spoonfuls of goop. Similarly, when they get tired, and ratty, and whiny, being a parent doesn't feel like the best decision you've ever made. About that time, it feels more like something you didn't quite think all the way through.

And if you approach the task with a grim, grey, earnest determination to squeeze every last possible developmentally stimulating experience you can from each moment, it's going to be a long, hard haul. Yes, you can count in Mandarin as each spoonful goes in — or you can make a small farty sound as each successful spoon hits the target. Which one sounds better for your long-term mental health?

As well as saving your own sanity, it's good for the wee people if the big ones loosen up and goof around a little. Research shows that happy people live longer than miserable ones. This is, I think, good news. After all, who really wants miserable people to enjoy a long life? There are all kinds of reasons for this difference in lifespan, but the bottom line is that having a positive attitude to life is a good thing. Humour is an important part of this. If you can laugh at the absurdities of yourself and the world in general, you're going to have a much easier time of it than someone who takes it all too seriously.

So, Goofing 101 for beginners. The first thing is random silliness. The more random and silly it is, the better. The random element is important, because most young children find unexpected things either terrifying or a bit of a laugh. If your goofing around is mostly terrifying them, that's a pretty good clue you might need to take it back a notch or two. Terror, generally, is a sign that you might have pushed things just that little bit too far.

It's a curious thing about us humans that we tend to laugh when unexpected things happen, but there you go. We don't need to speculate on what the evolutionary advantage might be of reacting with humour to unexpected events; we just need to exploit it. Peek-a-boo is one of the oldest tricks in the book, but for the tiny people it never fails to amuse.

Noise and suddenly moving a little one works wonders. For example, most two-year-olds will find it ridiculously funny to find themselves suddenly held upside-down by their ankles. Physical comedy is big with the littlies, so just think Charlie Chaplin meets the Teletubbies and you'll be in the ball park. Just take care not to scare them too much.

Here's a goofing-around starter pack to get you under way if goofing is not your natural thing. Just remember, there's an infinite number of ways to goof around — all you need is the will, and the way emerges quite naturally.

- Small farty noises. Even though very young children have yet to discover the full comic glory of the wee farty noise, it will still gain you some traction.
- General tossing in the air (with the usual blah-de-blah safety warnings about not chucking them too high, etc, etc). There's something about being thrown up in the air which pushes little funny buttons big time. For the really little ones, it's probably because they haven't discovered

gravity yet. For the older ones, it's in spite of the fact they understand gravity.

➼ Silly walks. If you're stuck for a silly walk, just Google it. The silly walk is a staple goofing-around tool and guaranteed to get a reaction.

➼ The purposeful missed dish. When you're serving their lunch, drop everything on the bench exactly 10 centimetres from their actual plate. Look confused as you drop each piece, as if you have no idea why it all keeps missing.

➼ Running away in terror. Every time they come up to you, simply turn and run away as though you're completely terrified. I don't know why this works, but it just does.

➼ The duck. Explain to them where you are going, and that they must put their shoes on, etc — except do it all by quacking.

➼ The inverted underpants. Tell them you are going to help them to get dressed and then put their underpants on their head. Works on a number of subtle comedic levels.

➼ The monkey on the table. Ask them to come and watch the monkey on the table with you. Describe in some detail the monkey's antics, as if you really were watching the monkey. Works just as well with a real monkey as an imaginary one.

➼ The talking control-freak stuffed toy. Choose their favourite stuffed toy, work it in a puppet-like fashion using a high-pitched voice with an Italian accent. Have the toy give them a number of sergeant-major-ish commands, such as sit down, stand up, sit down again, jump, keep jumping, keep jumping, sit down, jump sitting down, etc, etc. You can try other accents, but clinically I have found Italian to be the most effective.

➡ Narcolepsy. Now, while this is a serious medical condition which has devastating effects on the lives of its sufferers, it's also a great gag with pre-schoolers. All you do is fall asleep the instant they touch you, talk to you, look at you. Simple, but it gets them every time.

So that's all you need to know to get started. It's good for you, good for them, and most of all — it's fun. Just remember: don't get all serious about goofing off. Don't goof off because you feel like you'll be a bad parent if you don't, goof off when and if the goof takes you. It isn't yet another parenting task to add to the list, it's just a little bit of shim-sham to make the grind a little easier.

Have some fun.

40
The longest, shortest years of your life

Raising children takes anywhere from one to three eternities. Sunday afternoons in particular can stretch out to fill whole weeks all by themselves. Childless couples snooze, read books, and relax on a Sunday afternoon. Parents just try to survive it. You will want to do all those things, but they will no longer be possible. Snoozing, reading, and relaxing are for normal people, and you are not normal. You are a parent.

By the same token you should not go near normal people at these times, because the bitter resentment you feel over their aforementioned snoozing, reading, and relaxing may provoke you to acts of violence.

Raising children is something that takes over your life for what will feel like centuries. The time will drag. It will consume you until you can barely remember that there was ever a time before children, until you can barely remember your name. You will feel like this has been your life forever, that there was never a time when you were not wiping bottoms, cleaning up stains, being whined at, and building endless, tedious, precarious block towers.

You will feel that way for a hundred years at least, and then, one day, with no apparent warning, you will realize that all that is slipping away so fast you feel like you're falling. You will suddenly realize that your kids are growing up, that they are beginning to develop their own lives, their own friends, their own interests. They will need you less and less. They are beginning their own long trip, and increasingly you will just be a visitor along the way. Hard as it might be to believe right now, this will make you feel a dull, unformed sadness which starts in your belly and goes way down deep into the ground.

They are little for the longest, shortest time, so drink it deeply and fully. Make the most of it that you possibly can, get through on caffeine and sheer grit if you have to, because they will only be little for a blink. One day, much further away and sooner than you think, you will ache terribly for these precious, tedious, frustrating, joyful, spectacular, miraculous days. Don't wish it away, no matter how much you might want to, because just as you can't wish it away, you also can't wish it back. In years to come you will willingly pay a king's ransom just to see one last tantrum, to build one last stupid Lego tower, or read that one last bedtime story. Suddenly, when it's too late, one more story will not seem like such a big ask.

In the end the best piece of parenting advice that I can offer with any kind of certainty is this:

Enjoy.